Big Book of Monthly Arts & Crafts Primary

Table of Contents

About This Book

Big Book of Monthly Arts & Crafts
Primary

Whatever the season, you'll find just the arts-and-crafts activity you are looking for in this resource compiled of the best ideas from the Monthly Arts and Crafts series! For each month, we have included a collection of one-of-a-kind arts-and-crafts activities to add spark to your monthly thematic plans and ignite creativity in your students. Each activity includes a brief introduction to a theme, a quick and easy materials list, simple step-by-step instructions, a full-color illustration, and one or more teaching tips to help the activity go smoothly. Both teacher tested and kid approved, these arts-and-crafts activities will provide a year's worth of creative fun!

Managing Editor: Allison E. Ward

Editorial Team: Becky S. Andrews, Kimberley Bruck,
Karen P. Shelton, Diane Badden, Elizabeth H. Lindsay, Susan Walker,
Karen A. Brudnak, Sarah Hamblet, Hope Rodgers, Dorothy C. McKinney

Production Team: Lisa K. Pitts, Ivy L. Koonce (COVER ARTIST),
Pam Crane, Clevell Harris, Rebecca Saunders, Jennifer Tipton Bennett,
Chris Curry, Theresa Lewis Goode, Ivy L. Koonce, Clint Moore,
Greg D. Rieves, Barry Slate, Donna K. Teal, Tazmen Carlisle,
Amy Kirtley-Hill, Kristy Parton, Debbie Shoffner, Cathy Edwards Simrell,
Lynette Dickerson, Mark Rainey

www.themailbox.com

©2004 by The Mailbox®
All rights reserved.
ISBN# 1-56234-562-1

Manufactured in the United States
10 9 8 7 6 5 4 3 2 1

AUGUST

Melon Shaker

Create one juicy jamboree when each child uses his own watermelon shaker!

Materials (per child)

- heavy-duty 9" paper plate
- pink, brown, and green tempera paints
- paintbrushes
- 2–3 tbsp. dried beans
- stapler

Directions

1. Paint the back of the paper plate to resemble a watermelon.
2. Let the paint dry completely.
3. Fold the plate in half, painted side out.
4. Staple halfway around the plate's edge.
5. Pour the beans into the folded plate.
6. Staple the remaining edges closed.

Curriculum Connection
Music

Have your youngsters use their shakers to accompany this little ditty, sung to the tune of "Frère Jacques."

Watermelon, watermelon,
Tasty treat.
Tasty treat.
Juicy, juicy, juicy.
Juicy, juicy, juicy.
It's so sweet. It's so sweet.

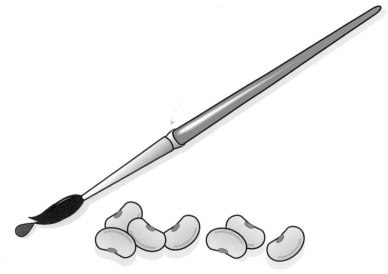

Amy Barsanti • Roper, NC

I Scream for Ice Cream!

Your youngsters are sure to scream over this "I-scream" project! Use the finished project to decorate your classroom.

Materials (per child)

- 6" x 12" sheet of brown construction paper
- four 3" white construction paper circles
- four 1" x 3" strips of cardboard
- assorted colors of tissue paper
- brown marker
- pencil
- scissors
- glue

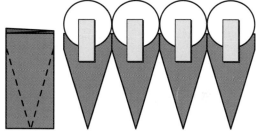

Directions

1. Accordion-fold the brown piece of paper into fourths.
2. Draw a cone shape on the folded paper as shown.
3. Carefully cut out the cone shape.
4. Unfold the paper and draw crisscross lines on the cones with the marker.
5. Glue a paper circle to the back of each cone.
6. For support, glue a cardboard strip to the back of each cone as shown.
7. Crumple the colored tissue into three-inch balls.
8. Glue each paper ball (ice cream) to the front of a white circle.

Curriculum Connection
Writing

Invite students to brainstorm words that describe ice cream. List their responses on a sheet of chart paper. Discuss other food items that might also match the same describing words.

Amy Barsanti • Roper, NC

Safari Binoculars

What do you spy? I spy a great set of safari binoculars!

Materials (per child)

- paper towel tube
- two 6-oz. foam cups
- brown and green tempera paints
- brown acrylic paint
- 3 paintbrushes
- 16" length of brown yarn
- hole puncher
- craft glue
- scissors

Directions

1. Cut the paper towel tube into two equal lengths.
2. Paint each tube brown. Let the paint dry.
3. Paint random green splotches on each tube, creating a camouflaged look. Let the paint dry.
4. Carefully cut out the bottom section of each cup. Then cut around the cup approximately one inch from the bottom.
5. Paint the resulting rings with the brown acrylic paint.
6. When the paint has dried, glue each ring to one end of each tube.
7. Glue the two tubes together as shown.
8. Punch a hole on either side of the binoculars, opposite the end with the rings.
9. Tie one yarn end through each hole in the tube.

Darcy Brown

Curriculum Connection
Social Studies

Display a large map of Africa. Divide students into groups of two or three. Have each group map out a route for an imaginary safari. Challenge each group to list what supplies it would need to bring on the safari. Ask each group to keep a log of what happens along the way.

Super Safari Hat

A safari wouldn't be complete without this hat!

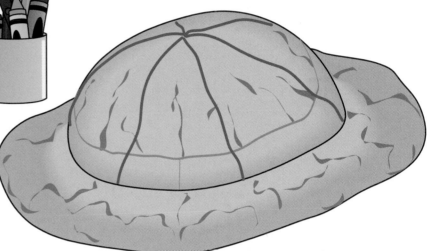

Materials (per child)

- 2 full sheets of newspaper
- partner
- masking tape
- tan tempera paint
- paintbrush
- brown marker

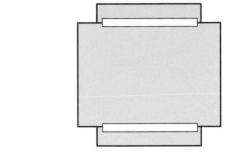

Directions

1. Tape the two sheets of newspaper together, forming a cross as shown.
2. Center the papers atop your head.
3. Have your partner tape the newspaper around your head at the brim.
4. Have your partner roll the outer edges of the paper inward and secure them with masking tape.
5. Slightly flatten the edges to form the brim of the hat.
6. Paint the brim (including the underside) and the top of the hat tan; then allow the paint to dry.
7. Decorate the hat with the marker as desired.

Susie Kapaun • Orchard Park, NY

Curriculum Connection
Language Arts

Ask each child to name a different safari animal. List the students' responses on the chalkboard. Then challenge each youngster to create a booklet page about an animal from the list, patterned after the classroom favorite *Brown Bear, Brown Bear, What Do You See?* by Bill Martin Jr. Have him complete the sentence "(Child's name, child's name), what do you see? I see a(n) (safari animal's name) looking at me!" Compile the finished pages into a class booklet.

Ladybug Pendant

Introduce your students to the beneficial ladybug with this easy-to-make pendant!

Materials (per child)

- plastic spoon
- petroleum jelly
- prepared plaster of paris
- small paper clip
- 2 wiggle eyes
- three 2½" pieces of black pipe cleaner
- red and black permanent markers
- 24" length of yarn
- glue

Directions

1. Lightly coat the bowl of the spoon with the petroleum jelly.
2. Carefully fill the spoon with the plaster of paris mixture.
3. Press the paper clip into the end of the mixture, leaving approximately one-fourth inch of the paper clip exposed. Allow the plaster to dry.
4. Remove the hardened plaster piece from the spoon.
5. Color ladybug features on the curved side of the plaster piece with the markers.
6. Glue the wiggle eyes to the head of the ladybug.
7. Glue the pipe cleaner pieces (legs) to the underside of the ladybug.
8. Thread the yarn length through the paper clip loop. Tie the ends of the yarn together.

Curriculum Connection
Writing

What good luck to find a ladybug in your garden! These beneficial bugs consume large quantities of plant pests, such as aphids. Challenge each child to write a letter to a ladybug that will persuade it to reside in her flower bed or garden.

Cynthia Holcomb • Mertzon, TX

Buzzing Bee

This little bee is taking care of some "bee-siness"!

Materials (per child)

- sterilized foam egg carton cup
- mini craft stick
- 2 small wiggle eyes
- green or clear flexible drinking straw
- 12" length of 18-gauge wrapped floral wire
- 1" x 3" piece of waxed paper (with the corners rounded)
- green tissue paper
- assorted tempera paints with dish soap added
- paintbrushes
- black permanent marker
- sharpened pencil
- scissors
- glue

Directions

1. Paint the egg cup a desired color; paint the craft stick yellow. Let the paint dry.
2. Poke a hole in the bottom of the egg cup (flower) with the pencil. Invert the flower and push the straw through the hole about 1½ inches. Squeeze glue around the straw to hold it in place; let the glue dry.
3. Fringe-cut the end of the straw inside the flower.
4. Use the marker to draw details on the yellow craft stick (bee).
5. Glue the wiggle eyes to the bee's head.
6. Twist the middle of the waxed paper to create wings. Glue the wings to the bee.
7. Bend one end of the wire to make a narrow hook. Glue the hook to the underside of the bee and bend the wire.
8. Insert the loose end of the wire into the straw; then loop the wire about one-half inch from the end.
9. Cut a small strip from the green tissue paper and tie it around the straw to resemble leaves. Glue it in place.

Curriculum Connection
Science

Have each child pull on the wire to simulate the bee pollinating the flower. Share the fact that honeybees carry out more cross-pollination than any other insect.

Mackie Rhodes • Greensboro, NC

Beach Prints

This adorable card will have your students dreaming of the beach!

Materials (per child)

- 5½" x 8½" piece of colored paper
- construction paper in assorted colors
- tempera paints
- shell
- beach grass
- shallow trays
- paintbrushes
- scissors
- glue

Directions

1. Cut or fold the colored paper to make a card.
2. Paint a thin coat of a desired color of paint on a tray.
3. Press the shell into the paint; then press the shell onto a scrap of construction paper.
4. Cut around the print, making a shell shape.
5. Repeat Steps 3 and 4 until a desired number of shells are made.
6. Glue the shell cutouts to the front of the card.
7. Paint another color of paint onto a different tray.
8. Press the beach grass onto the tray; then press the grass to the front of the card.
9. Repeat Step 8 as desired.

Curriculum Connection
Writing

Invite each child to write a personal message inside his handmade card. Encourage him to give his card to a loved one.

Amy Barsanti • Roper, NC

Sandpaper Castle

Here's a sand castle that will never wash away!

Materials (per child)

- sheet of sandpaper
- scissors
- glue
- 9" x 12" sheet of blue construction paper
- sand
- small shells
- cotton ball
- paintbrush
- pencil

Directions

1. Sketch a sand castle on the sheet of sandpaper.
2. Cut out the sand castle.
3. Glue the sand castle onto the blue paper.
4. Paint a thin layer of glue around the bottom of the sand castle.
5. Sprinkle sand atop the glue and shake off the excess.
6. Glue the shells around the sand castle.
7. Gently pull apart the cotton ball.
8. Glue the cotton ball wisps (clouds) above the sand castle.

Curriculum Connection
Science

Take your class outside to a large area, such as the playground. Then divide students into small groups. Provide each group with a container of water and a bucket of sand. Challenge each group to use the materials to construct an original sand castle.

Colleen Dabney • Williamsburg, VA

Flip-Flop Fun

You'll flip for these flip-flops!

Directions

1. Trace a left and a right shoe onto different sheets of construction paper.
2. Cut out each shoe shape and set it aside.
3. Press the cookie cutter into the craft foam twice.
4. Cut out the foam shapes along the indentations.
5. Decorate each foam shape with the paint pens.
6. Punch two holes in each foam shape.
7. Thread one ribbon through each foam shape and tie a bow.
8. Draw flip-flop features on each shoe.
9. Glue each foam shape to the top of a different shoe pattern.

Curriculum Connection
Math and Social Studies

Give small groups of students a map of your state or the United States. Have each group locate your hometown on the map. Challenge the students to use the map key to determine how many miles it will take them to flip-flop their way to the nearest beach.

Colleen Dabney • Williamsburg, VA

SEPTEMBER

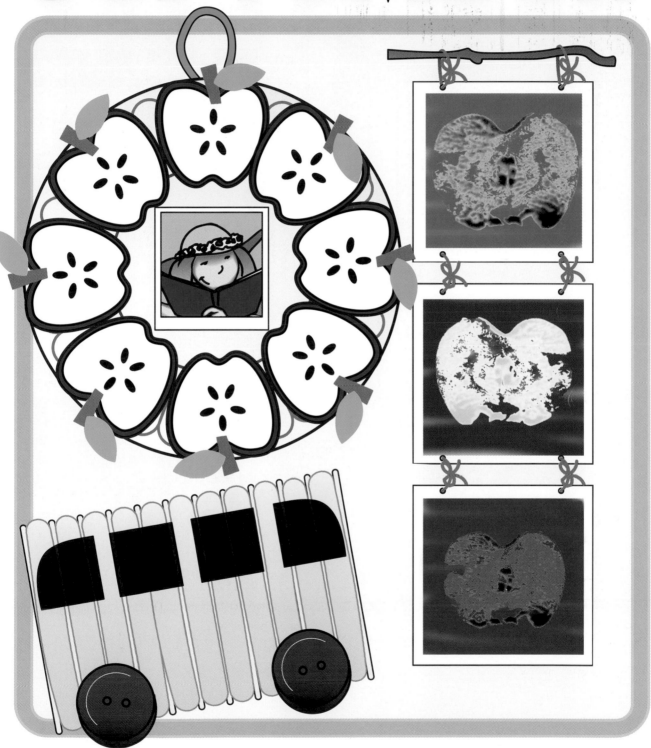

Perky Pencil Frame

Pencil these keepsake frames into your September plans.

Amy Barsanti • Roper, NC

Materials (per child)

- four 4 ½" craft sticks
- 4 ½" cardboard square
- yellow tempera paint
- paintbrush
- aluminum foil scraps
- photograph
- black and pink markers
- 3" strip of magnetic tape
- glue
- scissors

Directions

1. Draw a small triangle at one end of each craft stick to form a pencil point. Color the triangle black.
2. Color the other end of each craft stick pink to make an eraser.
3. Paint the middle of each craft stick yellow as shown. Let the paint dry.
4. Cut four small strips of foil. Glue each strip of foil beneath the eraser on each craft stick.
5. Glue the craft sticks to the cardboard square as shown.
6. Attach the magnetic tape to the back of the frame.
7. Glue a picture in the center of the frame.

Curriculum Connection
Math

Reinforce nonstandard units of measurement with craft-stick pencils! Have your students make several craft-stick pencils like the ones above. Challenge your youngsters to measure different items in the classroom using the pencils.

Crafty Crayons

These colorful crayons are as cute as can be!

Materials (per child)

- 4½" cardboard tube
- tempera paint
- paintbrush
- construction paper
- half of a 4" construction paper circle
- tape
- glue
- black marker
- scissors

Directions

1. Paint the tube a desired color. Let the paint dry.
2. Fold the paper half circle into a cone shape and secure it with a small piece of tape. Then tape the cone to the top of the tube.
3. Cut two ½" x 6" strips of construction paper and glue them around the top and bottom of the tube.
4. Cut arms and legs from the construction paper. Glue them to the tube as shown.
5. Draw facial features.
6. Write your name on the side of the crayon with a black marker.

Curriculum Connection
Language Arts

Open a box of 64 crayons and have students discuss the color names. Challenge each child to write a paragraph telling why a color was given a particular name. Display the writings near the crafty crayons.

Amy Barsanti • Roper, NC

Craft Stick Puzzle Art

Here's a puzzling way to turn a few craft sticks into a piece of art!

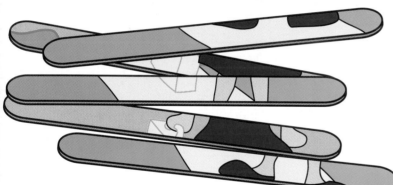

Materials (per child)

15 craft sticks
masking tape
markers or crayons
resealable plastic sandwich
  bag

Directions

1. Align the craft sticks side by side on a flat surface.
2. Place two strips of masking tape across the width of the combined sticks to secure them together.
3. Carefully turn over the connected craft sticks.
4. Use markers or crayons to illustrate a back-to-school scene on the sticks.
5. Remove the tape.
6. Scramble the pieces; then reassemble to re-create the artwork.
7. Store in the bag between uses.

Curriculum Connection
Social Studies

Promote interaction and social skills with this partner activity. Pair youngsters and ask them to solve one another's puzzles. Then, in a shared effort, let them try combining portions of both puzzles to create a unique scene.

Mary Rosenberg • Fresno, CA

"Personali-tee" Puzzle

Your new students will learn about one another as they take turns putting together their "personali-tee" puzzles!

Materials (per child)

- personalized construction paper copy of the T-shirt pattern on page 28
- gallon-size resealable plastic bag
- self-adhesive label
- scissors
- markers
- crayons

Directions

1. Before the first day of school, write each student's name in large letters across a different T-shirt pattern.
2. Give each child her personalized pattern.
3. Instruct each child to use markers and crayons to illustrate her T-shirt with some of her favorites, such as her favorite color, book, cartoon, food, hobby, pastime, pet, or movie.
4. Invite each child to introduce herself to her classmates by sharing her completed shirt.
5. Collect and laminate the T-shirts.
6. Write each child's name on a label and apply it to a plastic bag.
7. Cut each T-shirt into a four- or five-piece puzzle and store it in its matching bag when not in use.

Josephine Flammer • Bay Shore, NY

Curriculum Connection
Social Studies

Students will enjoy getting to know their classmates as they take turns assembling each other's puzzles. Place the puzzles at a center or another designated area in your classroom. Have a student select a puzzle and put it together. Provide time for each youngster to share one new thing she has learned about her friend.

A Bus for Us

These one-of-a-kind school buses are just what you need to enhance your transportation or bus safety unit!

Materials (per child)

2" x 3" piece of plastic cross-stitch canvas
yellow yarn
pin back (available at craft stores)
2 black buttons
black scrap of construction paper
masking tape
glue
scissors

Directions

1. Trim both long edges of the plastic canvas to expose the vertical canvas pieces.
2. Beginning at one end, wrap the yellow yarn around the canvas until it covers the entire piece, front and back.
3. Trim the yarn if needed. Then secure the yarn end to the back of the canvas with masking tape.
4. Glue on the buttons to form wheels, as shown.
5. Cut additional bus details from the black construction paper; glue them to the bus.
6. When the project has dried, glue a pin back to the back of the bus.

Amy Barsanti • Roper, NC

Curriculum Connection
Language Arts

To introduce bus safety, challenge small groups of youngsters to write their own versions of "The Wheels on the Bus." Provide time for each group to sing its verses to the class.

Grandparent Memories

These Grandparents Day memory books will touch both the young and young-at-heart!

Materials (per child)

- three 8 ½" squares of white paper
- 7" x 7" x 10" construction paper triangle
- glue
- markers
- photograph of grandparent(s) trimmed to 2" square

Figure 1

Figure 2

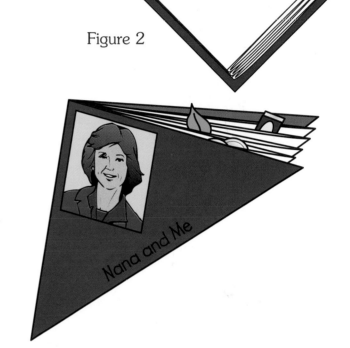

Nana and Me

Directions

1. Fold each of the white squares in half to form a triangle. Fold each triangle in half two more times to make progressively smaller triangles.
2. Unfold and flatten each piece.
3. Using the fold lines as a guide, refold each white square as shown in Figure 1.
4. Glue the white folded triangles atop one another.
5. Glue the stack of triangles atop the construction paper triangle as shown in Figure 2.
6. Fold the resulting stack in half to form the booklet.
7. Glue the photograph to the booklet cover. Use a marker to write the title "(Child's grandparent) and Me."
8. Illustrate each page of the booklet with a favorite memory and tuck small mementos into the pockets.

Curriculum Connection
Social Studies

Invite your students' grandparents to a Grandparents Tea. Provide muffins and tea (punch) for refreshments. During the tea, invite each child to share his memory booklet. Then have him present the booklet to his grandparent.

Amy Barsanti • Roper, NC

Apple Wreath

This "apple-rific" wreath is a great way to introduce your youngsters to apples!

Materials (per child)

- 8 red construction paper copies of the apple skin pattern on page 29
- 8 white construction paper copies of the apple fruit pattern on page 29
- brown and green construction paper scraps
- 9" paper plate
- 6" length of yarn
- photograph
- black marker or crayon
- glue
- scissors
- stapler

Directions

1. Cut out the red and white apple pieces.
2. Glue the red apple pieces around the rim on the back of the paper plate.
3. Glue the white apple pieces atop the red pieces.
4. Cut eight brown stems and eight green leaves from construction paper.
5. Glue the stems and leaves on the apples.
6. Draw five apple seeds on the middle of each apple as shown.
7. Glue the photograph to the middle of the plate.
8. When the project is dry, fold the yarn in half, knot the ends together, and staple it to the back of the plate for hanging.

Mary Rosenberg • Fresno, CA

Curriculum Connection
Social Studies

Celebrate the birth of Johnny Appleseed (September 26, 1774) with an apple-tasting party! Send a note home to parents requesting that various items made from apples (such as apple pie, apple-sauce, and caramel apples) be sent to school on a designated date. Invite students to taste the apple items. Then, if desired, have the students graph their favorites.

Hanging Apples

Bring a sign of the season into the classroom with these colorful apple banners!

Materials (per child)

- three 5" white poster board squares
- masking tape
- tempera paint in assorted colors
- paintbrush
- fresh apples (sliced in half)
- six 10" lengths of brown yarn
- hole puncher
- 7" twig

Directions

1. Tape lengths of masking tape around each posterboard square, creating a quarter-inch to half-inch border.
2. Paint each poster board square inside its tape border with a different color of paint.
3. After the paint has dried, carefully peel off the masking tape.
4. Paint the cut side of one apple half with a desired color of paint.
5. Press the apple onto one of the painted squares. Repeat the process for each remaining square. Let the paint dry.
6. Punch two holes at the top and bottom of two squares and at the top only on one square.
7. Tie the yarn lengths to assemble the project as shown.
8. Slide the small twig through the loops at the top of the banner for hanging.

Bette Munda • Athens, GA

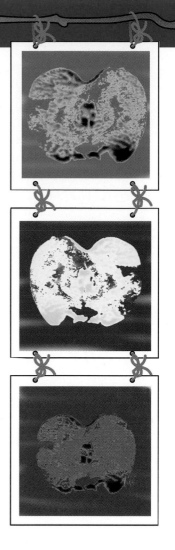

Curriculum Connection
Math

Students can explore symmetry with more apple prints! Have each youngster make an apple print on a sheet of white paper. Then have him fold his paper in half and press it together lightly. Direct him to unfold his paper. Discuss the symmetry in each special design.

Leaf Motif Notecard

Your students are sure to fall for this awesome autumn project!

Materials (per child)

foam vegetable tray
   sterilized and cut to 4" x 5 1/2"
5 1/2" x 8 1/2" white construction
   paper
pencil
tempera paint
paintbrush

Directions

1. Fold the white paper in half to make a notecard.
2. Use the pencil to draw a leaf design on the foam.
3. Brush a light coat of tempera paint over the design.
4. Press the painted design onto the notecard.
5. Carefully peel the notecard off the foam.
6. Allow the paint to dry completely.

Curriculum Connection
Language Arts

Reinforce letter-writing skills by having your youngsters write notes home to parents. Have each child pen a letter on the inside of his notecard. Challenge each student to include a fact or two he has learned about fall.

Amy Barsanti • Roper, NC

Corrugated Cardboard Art

These three-dimensional projects are sure to delight any youngster!

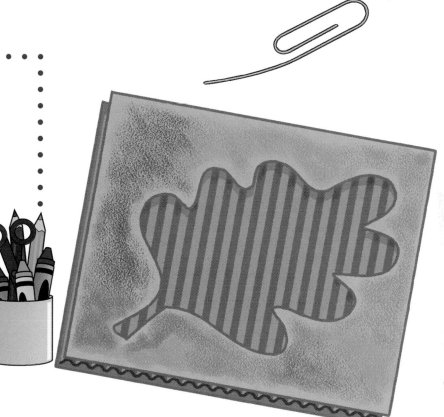

Materials (per child)

- 4" x 5" piece of corrugated cardboard
- large paper clip (unfolded at one end)
- access to sturdy templates of the leaf patterns on page 30
- access to sturdy templates of the fall patterns on page 31
- pencil
- crayons or markers

Directions

1. Select a leaf or fall pattern.
2. Use the pencil to trace the pattern onto the cardboard.
3. Use the paper clip to poke small holes close together along the traced design.
4. Gently peel away the top layer of paper inside the design to expose the corrugation.
5. Color the cardboard around the design as desired.

Curriculum Connection
Science

Take your youngsters on a leaf hunt! Invite each youngster to collect a variety of autumn leaves in a small paper bag. Ask him to sort his leaves by color, size, or variety. Then have each child write a few sentences about his findings. Display the writings near the corrugated art projects.

VaReane Gray Heese • Springfield, NE

Furry Squirrel

Your youngsters will flip over these furry squirrels!

Materials (per child)

white construction paper
   copy of the squirrel pattern
   on page 32
brown tempera paint
shallow pan
discarded toothbrush
scissors
half of a walnut shell
hot glue gun (for teacher
   use only)

Directions

1. Pour the paint into the pan.
2. Dip the toothbrush into the brown paint. Let the excess paint drip off into the pan.
3. Lightly brush the paint onto the squirrel in a circular motion.
4. Repeat Steps 2–3 until the entire squirrel has been painted.
5. Allow the paint to dry.
6. Cut out the squirrel along the bold outline.
7. Hot-glue the walnut shell where indicated. (Teacher step.)

Curriculum Connection
Social Studies

Involve your students in this fun gathering game. In advance, make 40 to 50 brown construction paper acorns (pattern on page 31). Hide the acorns around the classroom. Challenge groups of two or three students to quietly search the room and gather acorns. Then have each group count its findings. The group who gathers the most wins the round. Let the winning group hide the acorns for the next round of play.

Alyssa Weller • Skokie, IL

Leaf Person

These adorable leaf people will perk up any autumn classroom!

Materials (per child)

several items from nature, including a variety of leaves, small twigs, and seeds

9" x 12" sheet of orange construction paper

2 wiggle eyes

red marker

glue

Directions

1. Glue leaves to the paper to form a body and a head.
2. Trim small pieces of twigs for the arms and legs, and glue them to the paper.
3. Glue seeds or small leaves to form hands and feet.
4. Glue two wiggle eyes to the head and draw a smile.
5. Add additional items to the scene as desired.

Curriculum Connection
Math

Have each child count the number of nature items on his picture and write it in the corner of his paper. Pair students and have them add the two numbers. Have children switch partners several more times, stopping to calculate after each move.

Alyssa Weller • Skokie, IL

T-Shirt Pattern

Use with "'Personali-tee' Puzzle" on page 19.

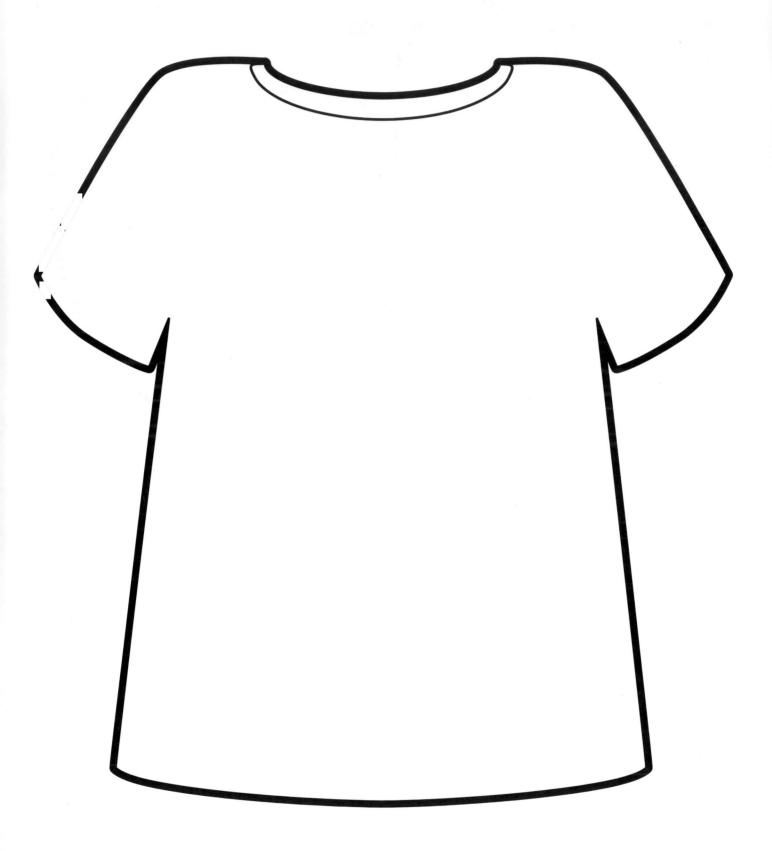

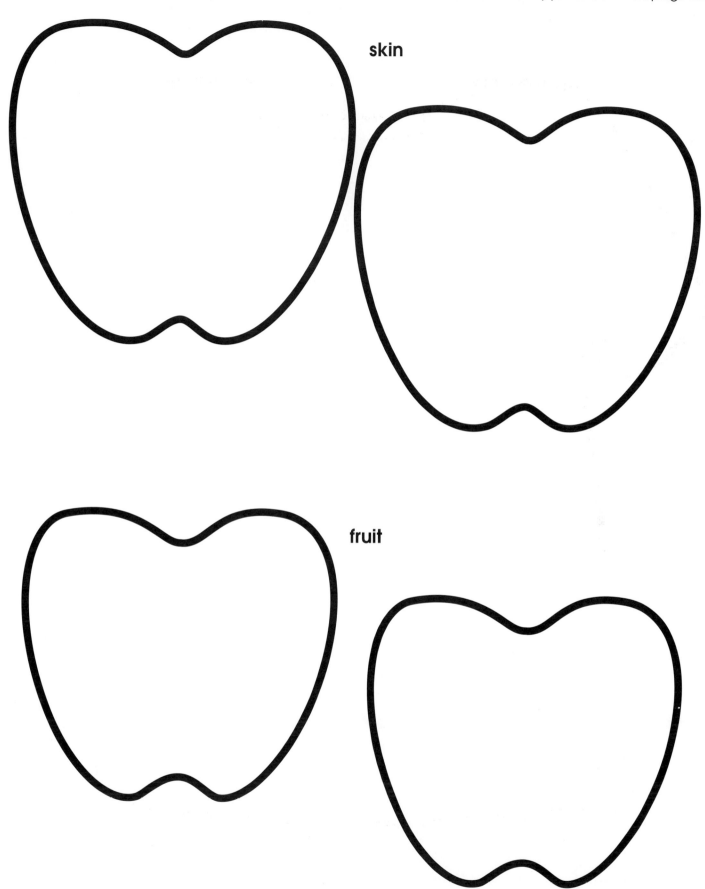

skin

fruit

Leaf Patterns

Use with "Corrugated Cardboard Art" on page 25.

Use with "Corrugated Cardboard Art" on page 25 and "Furry Squirrel" on page 26.

Squirrel Pattern
Use with "Furry Squirrel" on page 26.

Glue shell here.

OCTOBER

Leaf-Print Bookmark

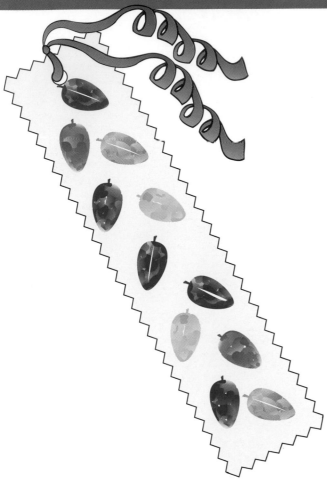

These bookmarks are sure to encourage your students to "leaf" through their favorite fall books!

Materials (per child)

- 2" x 8" piece of light-colored poster board
- variety of small, fresh leaves
- old newspapers
- brown, red, orange, and yellow tempera paints
- paintbrushes
- pinking shears or other "fancy-edged" scissors
- hole puncher
- 12" length of curling ribbon

Directions

1. Use the pinking shears to cut a fancy edge around the poster board.
2. Lay a sheet of newspaper over the workspace.
3. Paint one side of a leaf with paint.
4. Gently press the painted side of the leaf onto the piece of poster board.
5. Repeat with a variety of leaves and colors.
6. Punch a hole at the top of the bookmark.
7. Tie the curling ribbon through the hole.

Curriculum Connection Social Studies

Have your students create a leaf-print bookmark for distribution at a local care center. Have each child attach a short description of how the bookmark was made. Then plan a field trip for youngsters to present their special gifts.

Mary Richard • St. Augustine, FL

Can-Do Can

Spark your students' enthusiasm for fire safety with these tin can dalmatians!

Materials (per child)

- empty soup can with the label removed
- white and black acrylic paints
- paintbrush
- white construction paper
  copy of the small dog ear patterns on page 46
- black permanent marker
- glue
- scissors

Directions

1. Paint the outside of the can white. Let the paint dry.
2. Paint black spots on the outside of the can. Let the paint dry.
3. Cut out the ear patterns.
4. Use the marker to draw black spots on the ears.
5. Place glue on the tab along each ear.
6. Glue the ears to the side of the can.
7. Use the black marker to draw dog facial features on the front of the can.

Curriculum Connection
Social Studies

After discussing fire safety with your students, have them write tips they can follow in the event of a fire. Provide each student with five 2" x 6" strips of paper. Instruct each child to write a different fire safety tip on each strip. Have youngsters place their strips into their dalmatian cans as "can-do" reminders of fire safety!

Rebecca Brudwick • Mankato, MN

Set Sail With Columbus

In 1492, Columbus sailed the ocean blue.

Your youngsters are sure to set sail with Columbus when they create these nifty projects!

Materials (per child)

- paper plate
- drinking straw
- blue and purple construction paper in various shades
- white construction paper copy of the sail and Columbus patterns on page 47
- brown construction paper copy of the ship's bow pattern on page 47
- glue
- scissors
- crayons

Directions

1. Cut out the patterns.
2. Fold the ship's bow cutout down the middle. Unfold the bow and glue the sides to the middle of the plate, creating a pocket.
3. Cut slits along the dotted lines on the sail.
4. Slide the straw through the sail. Insert the straw into the bow.
5. Color the Columbus pattern and glue it just inside the top of the bow.
6. Tear the blue and purple construction paper into small pieces. Glue the pieces to the plate as shown.
7. Add desired crayon details to the plate.

Curriculum Connection
Social Studies

Invite small groups of students to work together to create timelines of the year 1492. Have each group research events that occurred in 1492. Ask them to select five events; then challenge each group to make a timeline on a length of bulletin board paper using text and drawings to describe each event.

Cindy Barber • Fredonia, WI

Pizza by the Slice!

This project looks almost good enough to eat!

Materials (per child)

- ⅙ of a paper plate
- orange and brown markers
- yellow crayon (with the label removed)
- scissors
- paintbrush
- glue
- construction paper scraps

Directions

1. Color the rim of the plate wedge brown.
2. Color the remaining part of the plate orange.
3. Paint a thin layer of glue over the orange section of the plate wedge.
4. Gently scrape the side of the yellow crayon with the scissors. Sprinkle the crayon shavings atop the glue.
5. Cut pizza toppings from the construction paper scraps. Glue the toppings to the pizza slice.

Curriculum Connection
Health

Ask each child to identify the food groups included on her pizza slice. Have her list the food-group items on a sheet of paper. Encourage students to compare the food groups found on their pizza slices.

Cynthia Holcomb • Mertzon, TX

Night Flier

Fashion these fluttery fliers for Halloween!

Materials (per child)

- 3-cup length of an empty, sanitized foam egg carton
- 5" x 8" piece of brown craft fur
- 3" square of brown felt or construction paper
- 2 wiggle eyes
- 2 brown 12" pipe cleaners
- brown tissue paper
- glue
- scissors
- stapler

10"

Directions

1. Drape the craft fur over the carton. Staple the fur to the sides of the carton and trim the edges.
2. Cut two 10-inch-long wing shapes from the tissue paper.
3. Beginning at the outside point of each wing, glue a pipe cleaner to the back of the curved part. (About an inch of pipe cleaner will overhang the wing at the wide end.)
4. Staple the exposed pipe cleaner end and the wing to the middle section of the egg carton. Repeat with the other wing.
5. Cut two ears and a small triangle from the brown felt.
6. Glue the ears to the top of the bat's head.
7. Glue the wiggle eyes and the triangle nose to the front of the bat's head.

Valerie Wood Smith • Morgantown, PA

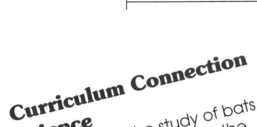

Curriculum Connection
Science

Swoop into the study of bats by helping students make the connection between the craft fur body and a bat's real fur. Explain that animals that have fur covering their bodies are mammals. Have the students name additional mammals. Challenge small groups of students to research how bats are unique among other mammals.

Spider Tie Puppet

Just wait till your youngsters get their hands on these adorable spider puppets!

Materials (per child)

- old necktie
- four 12" black pipe cleaners
- 2 wiggle eyes
- 2" length of red pipe cleaner
- scissors
- glue

Directions

1. Cut the tie approximately eight inches from the wide, pointed end.
2. Bend the black pipe cleaners, as shown, to form legs.
3. Glue the legs to the back of the tie. Let the glue dry completely.
4. Bend the red pipe cleaner to form a smile.
5. Glue the smile and the wiggle eyes to the front of the tie.
6. Slip your hand into the tie's opening to maneuver the puppet.

Curriculum Connection
Language Arts

Divide students into small groups. Challenge each group to write a short puppet skit about spiders. Invite each group to present its play to the class while using the spider puppets.

Amy Barsanti • Roper, NC

Spooky Shadows

Youngsters will proudly display these shadowed silhouettes!

Materials (per child)

- 9" x 12" sheet of orange construction paper
- 9" x 12" sheet of yellow construction paper
- 4" x 8" piece of black construction paper
- template of the bat pattern on page 48
- black tempera paint
- drinking straw
- plastic spoon
- pencil
- scissors
- glue

Directions

1. Leaving one long side, trim to round the yellow construction paper into a half-moon shape.
2. Glue the moon to the orange construction paper as shown.
3. Trace the bat pattern onto the black construction paper.
4. Cut out the bat and glue it so that it overlaps the yellow and orange sections.
5. Spoon a small amount of the black paint along the bottom of the picture.
6. Use the straw to blow the paint toward the center of the paper.

Curriculum Connection
Language Arts and Science

Invite each child to write a limerick (or a five-lined poem) about his picture. Mount each poem on orange construction paper. Display the poems below the projects for a "spook-tacular" display!

VaReane Gray Heese • Omaha, NE

Growing Monster

This little monster is sure to delight any youngster!

Directions

1. Paint the cup with a desired color of paint. Let the paint dry.
2. Cut monster face details from the construction paper scraps and glue them to one side of the cup.
3. Fill the cup with potting soil.
4. Sprinkle grass seed on the soil.
5. Water the grass seed as needed.

Curriculum Connection
Science

Challenge students to keep daily plant diaries. Have each youngster staple drawing paper between two construction paper covers and decorate the front cover as desired. Direct each child to keep a daily record of the growth of his grass seed. Have him draw a picture and write a sentence about his daily findings.

Cindy Barber • Fredonia, WI

"Boo-tiful" Windsock

An autumn breeze will set this beautiful windsock aflutter!

Materials (per child)

- 9" x 12" sheet of black construction paper
- construction paper copies of assorted Halloween patterns from pages 48 and 49
- colored glue or puff paint
- five 12" strips of yellow crepe paper
- 8" length of yarn
- glue
- hole puncher
- stapler
- scissors

Directions

1. Cut out the Halloween shapes and glue them to the black construction paper.
2. Use the colored glue to add seasonal phrases. Let the glue dry.
3. Bend the paper into a tube and staple the short edges together.
4. Glue the crepe paper strips inside the bottom edge of the tube.
5. Punch two holes at either side of the top edge.
6. Tie the yarn ends through the holes.

Curriculum Connection
Science

On a windy day, take your class outside and have each youngster drop a small, lightweight object, such as a feather or a slip of paper. Have each child determine the direction in which the object blew. Using that information, have her determine the direction from which the wind is blowing.

Margaret Southard • Cleveland, NY

"Whoooo" Is It?

It will be a hoot trying to guess who is hidden behind these fine-feathered masks!

Materials (per child)

- tagboard copy of the mask pattern on page 49
- yellow construction paper copy of the beak patterns on page 49
- various fall shades of felt or tissue paper
- unsharpened pencil
- glue
- scissors
- packing tape

Directions

1. Cut feather shapes from the felt or tissue paper and glue them to the mask.
2. Cut out the beak patterns and fold them along the dotted lines.
3. Glue the tabs of the larger beak pattern to the nose area of the mask.
4. Glue the smaller beak pattern inside the upper beak as shown.
5. Tape the pencil to one side of the back of the mask.

Curriculum Connection
Science

Most owls are known to be night hunters. Delve into the nocturnal world by inviting students to investigate other creatures of the night. Provide a variety of research materials. Challenge each youngster to write a report about his findings.

Valerie Wood Smith • Morgantown, PA

Jazzy Jack-o'-Lantern

Watch your classroom light up with these jazzy jack-o'-lanterns!

Materials (per child)

- copy of the pumpkin pattern on page 50
- 9" x 12" piece of tagboard
- assorted crayons, including black
- scissors
- wooden craft stick
- pencil

Directions

1. Trace the pumpkin pattern onto the tagboard.
2. Cut out the tagboard pumpkin.
3. Color the pumpkin heavily with a variety of bright-colored crayons.
4. Using a black crayon, color a heavy layer over the top of the colored crayon layer.
5. Use the craft stick to gently scrape away the black crayon to create jack-o'-lantern facial features.

Curriculum Connection
Health and Safety

Invite students to discuss Halloween safety rules. Provide each student with a white construction paper cutout of the pumpkin pattern on page 50. Instruct each youngster to write and illustrate a Halloween safety rule on his paper. Compile the pumpkins into a booklet to read prior to Halloween.

VaReane Gray Heese • Omaha, NE

Puffy Pumpkin

This adorable take-home treat is sure to perk up any student's Halloween!

Materials (per child)

- paper lunch sack
- discarded newspapers
- rubber band
- 24" length of green crepe paper
- popped popcorn
- shallow dishes of orange and brown tempera paint
- 2 cotton balls
- clothespin
- black construction paper scraps
- glue
- scissors

Directions

1. Open the lunch sack and place it atop a sheet of newspaper.
2. Clip a cotton ball to the clothespin.
3. Dip the cotton in brown paint, and then use it to sponge-paint the top three inches of the bag.
4. Using the clothespin, a fresh cotton ball, and orange paint, sponge-paint the remaining unpainted surface of the bag. Let the paint dry.
5. Cut a jack-o'-lantern mouth, nose, and eyes from the black construction paper and glue them to one side of the bag.
6. Fill the bag three-fourths full with popped popcorn.
7. Secure the top of the bag with a rubber band.
8. Tie the length of crepe paper around the banded area.

Cynthia Holcomb • Mertzon, TX

Curriculum Connection Math

Pumpkin seeds are planted in groups called hills. The pumpkins are ready to harvest in 120 days, usually before the first frost. After sharing this fact with your students, ask them to calculate the approximate harvest date of pumpkins if they were planted today.

Small Dog Ear Patterns
Use with "Can-Do Can" on page 35.

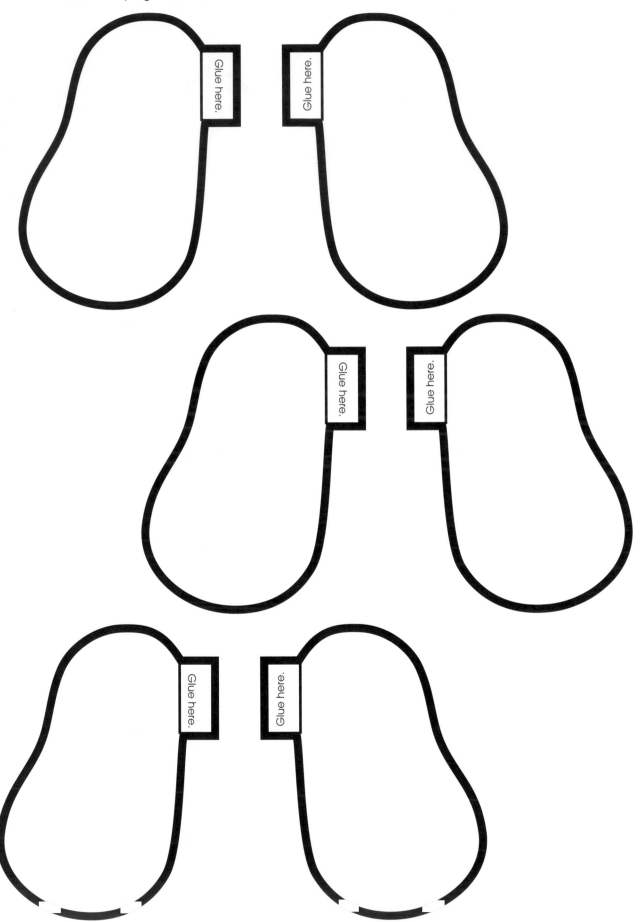

Glue here.

Glue here.

Glue here.

Glue here.

Glue here.

Glue here.

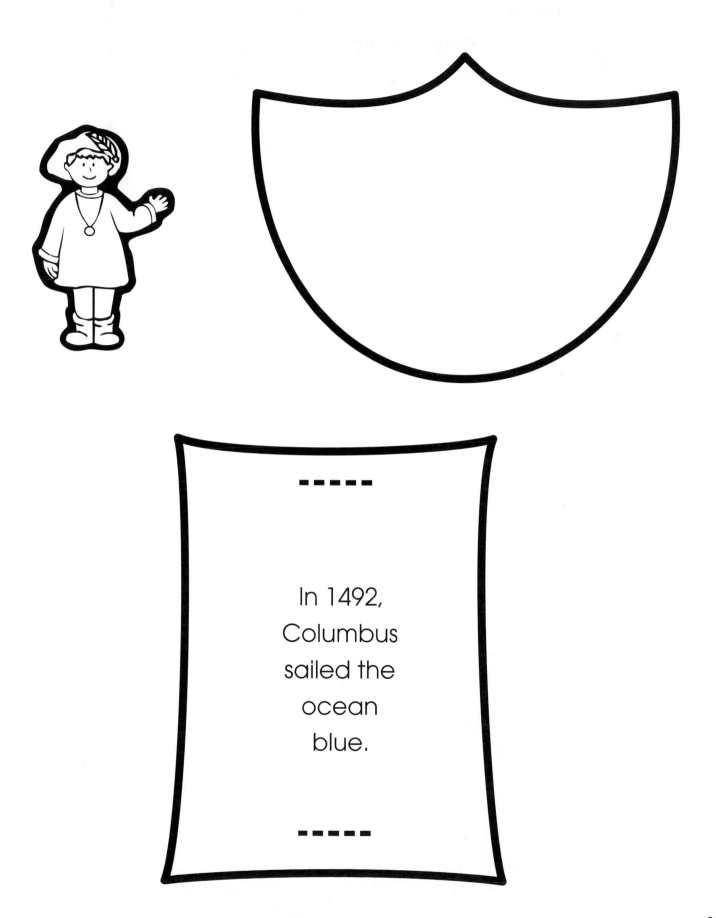

In 1492,
Columbus
sailed the
ocean
blue.

Halloween Patterns

Use the bat pattern with "Spooky Shadows" on page 40.
Use with " 'Boo-tiful' Windsock" on page 42.

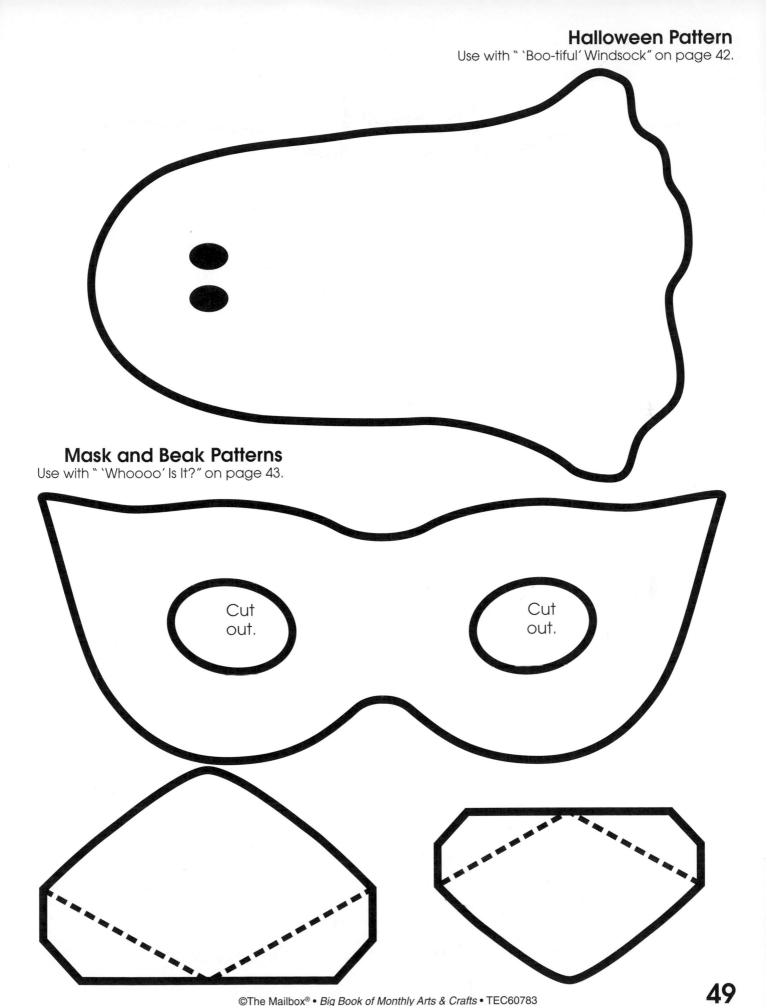

Mask and Beak Patterns
Use with " 'Whoooo' Is It?" on page 43.

Cut out.

Cut out.

Pumpkin Pattern
Use with "Jazzy Jack-o'-Lantern" on page 44.

NOVEMBER

Election Day Badge

These Election Day badges are sure to remind your youngsters' family members to vote!

Materials (per child)

- small plastic lid (approximately 3" diameter)
- copy of the badge pattern on page 62
- red, white, or blue chenille pipe cleaner
- crayons
- scissors
- star stickers
- glue
- ½" x 18" red, white, or blue ribbon
- safety pin

Directions

1. Color and cut out the badge pattern.
2. Decorate the badge with star stickers.
3. Glue the pipe cleaner around the outside edge of the lid.
4. Glue the badge atop the lid and pipe cleaner.
5. Fold the ribbon as shown and glue it to the back of the lid.
6. Attach the safety pin to the ribbon.

Curriculum Connection
Social Studies

Challenge your class to nominate students for classroom helpers. Each day invite a different nominee to state why she thinks she would make a good classroom helper. Throughout the week, have your students wear their badges as reminders to vote. At the end of the week, have each youngster vote for a classroom helper.

Penny Stephens • Greensboro, NC

Bookworm Mobile

This darling dangler is sure to inspire your youngsters during National Children's Book Week, celebrated annually during the week before Thanksgiving!

Materials (per child)

- wire clothes hanger
- 2" x 18" sheet of light-colored construction paper
- 9" x 12" sheet of green construction paper
- construction paper scraps
- hole puncher
- scissors
- 5 pieces of yarn in varied lengths
- 5 copies of the book pattern on page 63
- glue
- crayons

Directions

1. Fold the large sheet of construction paper over the bottom of the hanger. Wrap it around the hanger until it is covered. Glue the paper in place; then trim it as needed.
2. Cut six three-inch circles from the green construction paper and glue them to the paper on the hanger to form a bookworm.
3. Cut worm features from the construction paper scraps and glue them in place.
4. Write a different favorite book title on each book pattern and draw a picture from each story on the corresponding pattern. Then cut out the patterns.
5. Punch five holes along the bottom of the hanger.
6. Punch one hole at the top of each book pattern.
7. Tie each book to the hanger using a length of yarn.

Cynthia Holcomb • Mertzon, TX

Curriculum Connection
Language Arts

Take your class on a walking tour of your school library. Explain to your youngsters how to locate books on a library shelf. Challenge each youngster to locate each book he illustrated on his mobile.

Terrific Turkey

This showstopping headband is sure to be the hit of your Thanksgiving festivities!

Materials (per child)

- 2 yellow, 2 red, and 2 orange construction paper copies of the feather pattern on page 63
- two 2" x 12" brown construction paper strips
- white, red, and yellow construction paper scraps
- scissors
- stapler
- markers
- glue

Directions

1. Staple the brown strips together at one end. Size it to your head and staple the remaining ends to form a headband. Cut off any excess after stapling.
2. Cut out the feathers and glue them to one side of the headband.
3. Cut eyes, a beak, and a wattle from construction paper.
4. Glue the turkey facial features to the headband as shown.
5. Use a marker to make additional details on the headband.

Curriculum Connection
Social Studies

Native Americans first introduced the Pilgrims to wild turkeys as a source of food. As a tradition, families eat turkey on Thanksgiving. Invite each student to share one of his family's Thanksgiving traditions.

Valerie Wood Smith • Morgantown, PA

54

Quirky Turkey Magnet

Gobble up this craft full of feathery fun—your youngsters will be glad you did!

Materials (per child)

- wooden ice-cream spoon
- craft feathers
- 2 wiggle eyes
- orange and red construction paper scraps
- 1" piece of magnetic tape
- scissors
- glue

Directions

1. Glue the craft feathers to one side of the wooden spoon to create a turkey.
2. Glue the wiggle eyes to the spoon as shown.
3. Cut a beak, feet, and a wattle from the construction paper scraps and glue them to the turkey.
4. Adhere the magnetic tape to the back of the turkey.

Curriculum Connection
Science

Provide a variety of real feathers for students to examine. Have your youngsters compare and contrast the real feathers to those used in the project. Invite each child to name one way the feathers are alike and one way they are different.

Amy Barsanti • Roper, NC

Ice-Cream Cone Cornucopia

This cornucopia looks good enough to eat!

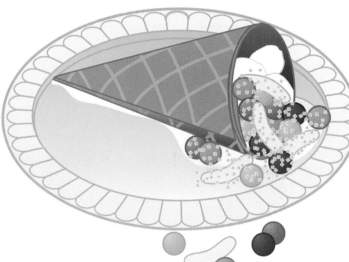

Materials (per child)

- 6" paper plate
- sugar ice-cream cone
- cotton balls
- Fruit Runts candies
- gold glitter
- craft glue

Directions

1. Fill the ice-cream cone with cotton balls.
2. Glue the ice-cream cone to the middle of the plate.
3. Glue a pile of candies over and near the opening of the cone.
4. Sprinkle the candies with gold glitter.

Curriculum Connection
Social Studies

The cornucopia is a symbol of abundance, meaning that it will always be plentiful and full of food. After sharing this fact with your students, have each child brainstorm what food items she would like to have in a cornucopia of her own. Invite each child to illustrate her cornucopia.

Betsy Gaynor • Naperville, IL

Thanksgiving Name Card

Decorate your students' desks with these Thanksgiving name cards!

Directions

1. Fold the construction paper into thirds. Unfold.
2. Trace a name card pattern onto the paper so that it overlaps the top and middle sections as shown.
3. Cut along the portion of the tracing that extends onto the top third only.
4. Twist a square of tissue paper around the eraser end of the pencil.
5. Dip the eraser end into glue and apply it to the traced shape.
6. Repeat Steps 4 and 5 until the entire shape is covered with tissue squares.
7. Write your name in marker on the name card.
8. Fold back a half-inch of the bottom third.
9. Fold the top third back and glue it to the half-inch fold to create a standing sign.

VaReane Gray Heese • Springfield, NE

Curriculum Connection
Language Arts

Challenge your youngsters to practice their alphabetizing skills. Have a small group of students hold their name cards and stand in front of the class. Invite the other youngsters to direct the children to stand in ABC order according to their names. Repeat with a new set of students until every child has had a turn.

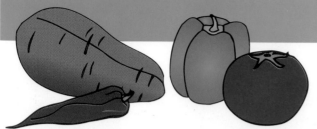

Veggie Quilt

Sew up this crazy, colorful quilt to remind everyone to eat their vegetables!

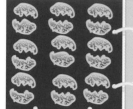

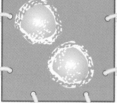
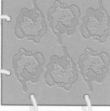

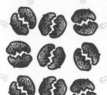
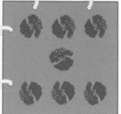

Directions

1. Paint the flat side of a vegetable with a desired color.
2. Press the vegetable onto a square.
3. Repeat the printing process to create patterns.
4. Punch two evenly spaced holes on the edges of each square.
5. Use yarn to tie the squares together.

Curriculum Connection
Health

Clean the unused vegetables and cut them into small pieces. Place them in a pot with water and place them on a heat source until boiling, stirring occasionally. Drain the water. Add prepared chicken broth to the vegetables and simmer over low heat until the vegetables are tender. Serve the soup to your youngsters.

Bette Munda • Athens, GA

Colonial Cross-Stitch Sampler

Invite your youngsters to step back in time as they create these crafty cross-stitch samplers!

Materials (per child)

- copy of the colonial sampler pattern on page 64
- 9" x 12" sheet of brown construction paper
- colored markers or crayons
- pencil
- glue

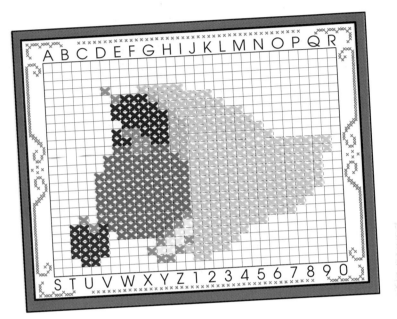

Directions

1. Lightly pencil a Thanksgiving or fall design by drawing Xs on the grid.
2. Trace over the Xs with markers.
3. Glue the sampler to the construction paper to frame the design.

Curriculum Connection
Math

Invite a quilter or cross-stitcher to speak to your youngsters. Ask her to bring samples of her work. Challenge students to discuss the patterns found in the handicrafts.

Cindy Barber • Fredonia, WI
VaReane Gray Heese • Springfield, NE

Pioneer Rag Doll

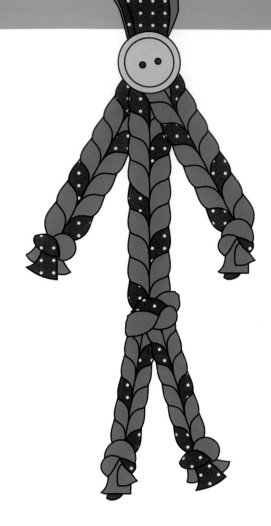

These handmade pioneer pals will delight any youngster!

Materials (per child)

- six 1" x 12" strips of cotton fabric in different colors
- three 1" x18" strips of cotton fabric in different colors
- 4" piece of yarn
- large button
- masking tape
- hot glue gun (for teacher use only)
- scissors

Directions

1. Stack the strips in random order on top of one another, aligning one end.
2. Tie the yarn tightly around the nine strips two inches from the aligned end.
3. Use masking tape to tape the tied end to a desk to hold it in place.
4. Braid three of the short strands together to make an arm; repeat with the other three strips.
5. Tie a knot at the end of each arm to secure.
6. Braid the three remaining long strands to within six inches of the bottom and knot.
7. Carefully cut the remaining portion of the strips up the middle lengthwise.
8. Braid these new strips into two sets of three for legs and knot them at the ends.
9. Remove the tape; then hot-glue the button head to the top of the braids just above the yarn. (The teacher should perform this step.)

VaReane Gray Heese • Springfield, NE

Curriculum Connection
Social Studies

Invite each child to interview an older relative or neighbor to find out what types of toys he or she played with as a child. Challenge each youngster to decide how the toys are similar to or different from the toys of today.

Snow Snake

Replicate a part of Native American history by making these decorative snow snakes.

Materials (per child)

- 2"-wide dowel or branch, cut into a 1' length
- sandpaper
- towel
- fabric or acrylic paints
- paintbrush

Directions

1. Sand the dowel to remove the rough edges.
2. Rub the towel over the dowel to remove the dust.
3. Paint Native American designs on the dowel.

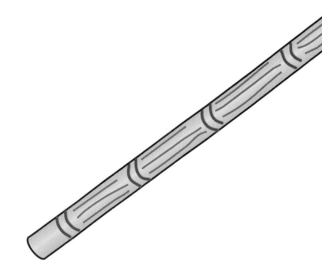

Curriculum Connection
Social Studies

Snow snake was a game played by Native Americans. The "snakes" were made out of wood and were from five to nine feet long. The players slid the snow snakes down a snow-packed track. The person who slid the "snake" the farthest was determined the winner.

VaReane Gray Heese • Springfield, NE

Badge Pattern
Use with "Election Day Badge" on page 52.

Name Card Patterns
Use with "Thanksgiving Name Card" on page 57.

Don't Forget to ☆ VOTE! ☆

Book Pattern
Use with "Bookworm Mobile" on page 53.

Feather Patterns
Use with "Terrific Turkey" on page 54.

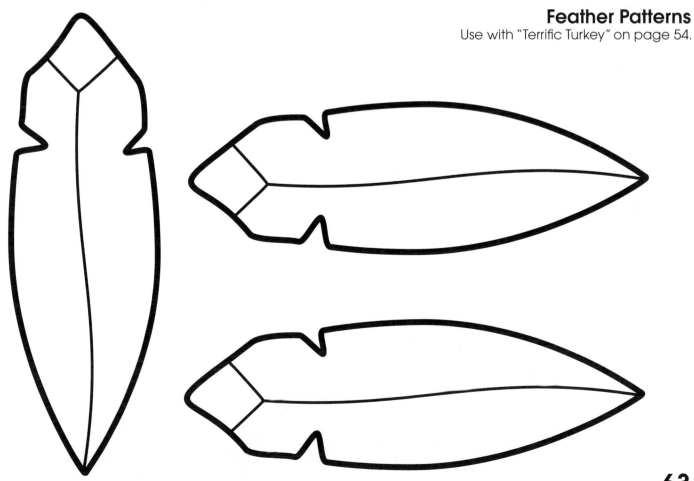

Colonial Sampler Pattern

Use with "Colonial Cross-Stitch Sampler" on page 59.

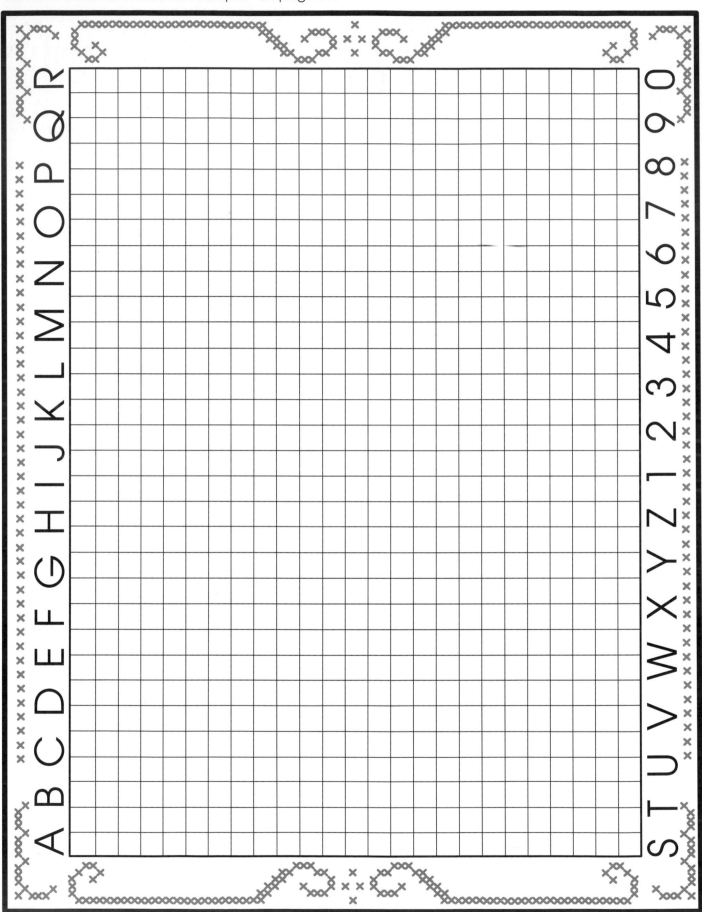

DECEMBER

Ginger Kids

This sweet treat of a craft looks like gingerbread and can be made in a snap!

Materials (per child)

- 6" x 6" square of brown or tan felt
- small rickrack
- assorted sequins
- 5" piece of yarn
- scissors
- glue

Directions

1. Cut a gingerbread boy or girl shape from the brown felt.
2. Cut the rickrack to appropriate lengths to fit the gingerbread child as shown.
3. Glue the rickrack in place.
4. Glue on sequins to form a mouth, eyes, and nose.
5. Loop the yarn and glue it to the back of the gingerbread child to form a hanger.

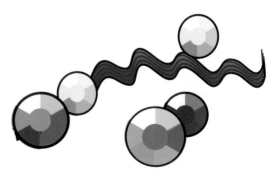

Curriculum Connection
Math

Bring in a variety of ginger-based food products, such as ginger-snap cookies and gingerbread. Invite each youngster to taste each of the products and determine a favorite. As a class, graph the results of the taste test.

Amy Barsanti • Roper, NC
Mary Rosenberg • Fresno, CA

Dazzling Dreidel Decoration

Display this dazzling dreidel during Hanukkah!

Materials (per child)

- two 5" squares of clear Con-Tact covering
- 12" blue pipe cleaner
- blue and gold glitter
- 6" length of white ribbon
- scissors
- hole puncher

Directions

1. Lay one piece of Con-Tact covering sticky side up.
2. Bend the pipe cleaner into a dreidel shape.
3. Press the shape to the Con-Tact covering.
4. Sprinkle glitter onto the Con-Tact covering inside the pipe cleaner shape.
5. Press the other piece of Con-Tact covering, sticky side down, atop the first.
6. Trim the edges of the paper around the dreidel.
7. Punch a hole at the top of the dreidel.
8. Thread the ribbon through the hole and tie.

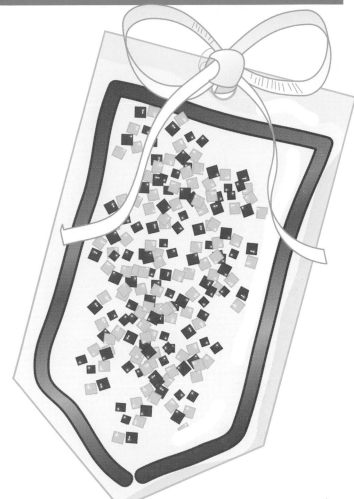

Curriculum Connection
Social Studies

Invite your students to investigate dreidels. Provide students with a variety of research materials related to Hanukkah. Have each child use the materials to write a report about this traditional Hanukkah game.

Darcy Brown

Magnificent Menorah

This magnificent menorah is sure to brighten your Hanukkah holiday!

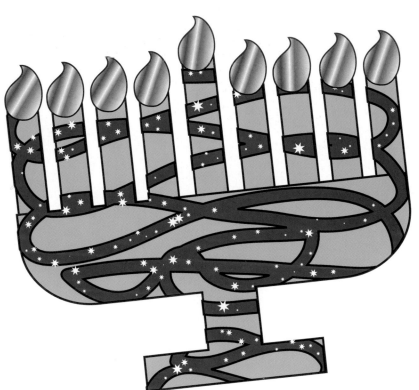

Materials (per child)

9" x 12" sheet of blue
  construction paper
eight 1" x 5" strips of blue
  construction paper
1" x 6" strip of blue
  construction paper
sheet of newspaper
blue or silver glitter
aluminum foil
glue
scissors

Directions
1. Cut a menorah shape from the sheet of blue construction paper.
2. Glue the nine blue strips to the menorah as shown to form candles.
3. Lay the menorah on a sheet of newspaper to protect the workspace.
4. Drizzle glue atop the menorah.
5. Sprinkle blue or silver glitter atop the glue. Let it dry.
6. Cut nine flames from the foil.
7. Glue the flames atop the candles.

Curriculum Connection
Writing

Challenge each student to write an acrostic poem about Hanukkah. Have each youngster write "MENORAH" vertically along the left side of a sheet of paper. Then instruct him to write one word or descriptive phrase about Hanukkah following each letter. Display the writings near the projects.

Darcy Brown

Kwanzaa Flag

Making these fabulous flags is the perfect way for your students to celebrate Kwanzaa!

Materials (per child)

- 6" x 9" piece of black construction paper
- 3" x 9" strip of green construction paper
- 3" x 9" strip of red construction paper
- 10" wooden skewer (with the point removed)
- scissors
- glue

Directions

1. Cut a wavy edge along one long side of the red construction paper strip.
2. Glue the strip to the black construction paper as shown.
3. Cut a wavy edge along one long side of the green construction paper strip.
4. Glue this strip to the black construction paper as shown.
5. Glue the wooden skewer to the back of the flag as shown.

VaReane Gray Heese • Omaha, NE

Curriculum Connection
Social Studies

Have students use a variety of research materials to learn more about countries or holidays that have a flag as a symbol. Invite each child to draw a picture of her favorite flag to share with the class.

Shape Kinara

Kwanzaa's coming! Get in shape for the celebration with these geometric creations.

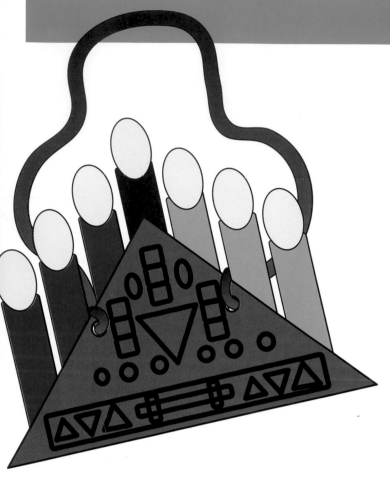

Directions

1. Glue the black construction paper strip behind the top point of the triangle.
2. Glue the red construction paper strips along the left side of the triangle, spacing them evenly.
3. Glue the green construction paper strips along the right side of the triangle, spacing them evenly.
4. Cut seven small ovals from the yellow construction paper.
5. Glue each oval flame atop a different construction paper strip.
6. Use the crayons to decorate the front of the project with geometric shapes.
7. Punch one hole on each side of the project as shown.
8. Thread an end of the yarn through each hole and tie to secure.

Curriculum Connection
Writing

Kwanzaa is based on seven principles. The kinara, lit during Kwanzaa, has seven candles—the black candle represents Black Americans, the three red candles symbolize past and present struggles, and the three green candles represent hope for the future. Challenge each child to write about how he feels about his hope for the future. Invite each youngster to share his writing with his classmates.

Cynthia Holcomb • Mertzon, TX

What's in the Box?

What better gift to give than one that comes from the heart?

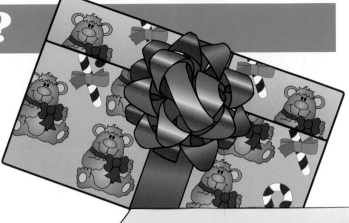

Materials (per child)

- 9" x 12" sheet of sturdy holiday wrapping paper or decorative wallpaper
- 12" length of ribbon
- package bow
- photograph
- glue

Directions

1. Glue the length of ribbon vertically down the middle of the paper's decorated side.
2. Turn the paper over.
3. Fold down one inch of the top edge.
4. Fold up the bottom to touch the top fold.
5. Open the folds and glue the photograph to the inside of the project.
6. Refold the larger flap and tuck it under the smaller one.
7. Press the bow to the two flaps to hold them together.

My mom is very special to me. She takes care of me. She helps me. I love my mom.

Curriculum Connection
Writing

Before students seal their gifts with the bow, invite each youngster to write about a special person in her life. Have the child pen her thoughts on the inside of her project, beneath her photograph. Ask the student to present her gift to that special person.

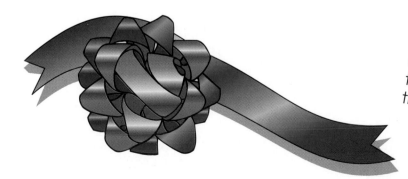

Cindy Barber • Fredonia, WI

Christmas Flower

This colorful project adds a festive touch to the traditions of Christmas.

Materials (per child)

- red construction paper copy of the leaf patterns on page 81
- green construction paper copy of the leaf patterns on page 82
- 1" yellow construction paper circle
- large paper fastener
- hole puncher
- scissors

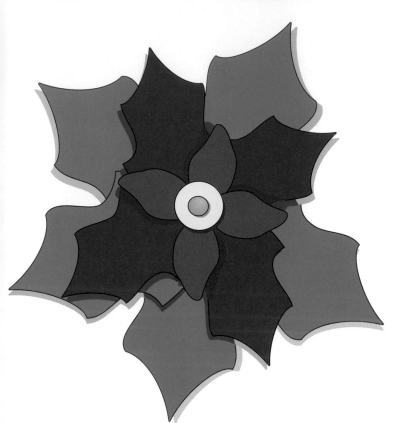

Directions

1. Cut out the red leaf patterns and sort them by size.
2. Cut out the green leaf patterns.
3. Punch a hole through the ● on each leaf pattern and through the center of the yellow construction paper circle.
4. Thread the paper fastener through the hole in the yellow circle.
5. Thread the paper fastener through the holes in the small red leaves, the large red leaves, and then the green leaves.
6. Open the paper fastener prongs to secure the flower pieces together.
7. Spread the leaves to form a flower.

Curriculum Connection
Science
Have students research how poinsettias grow. Invite each child to write a report about his findings. Display the writings near the poinsettia flowers.

Beverly McCormick Peerson • Signal Mountain, TN

Sparkle Tree

Wind this sparkly tree into your holiday ornament-making plans!

Materials (per child)

- green pipe cleaner
- assorted sequins
- glue

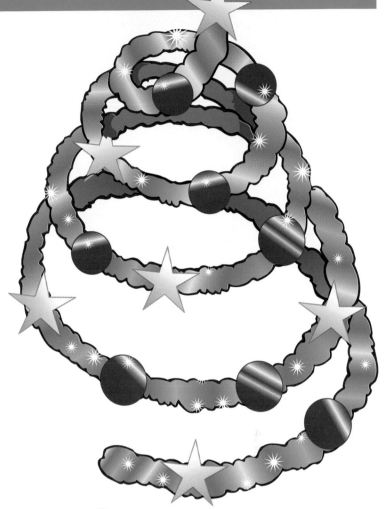

Directions

1. Wind the pipe cleaner into a spiral.
2. Gently pull up on the inner portion of the spiral to make a tree shape as shown.
3. Glue the sequins (ornaments) to the tree.

Curriculum Connection
Math

Ask students to name holiday decorations they use at their homes. Create a bar graph outline on a large sheet of poster board. Label the graph with the students' responses. Then write a title on the top of the graph. Have each youngster write her name on self-sticking notes and place them next to the categories on the graph which describe the decorations in her house. Discuss the resulting graph with the students.

Amy Barsanti • Roper, NC

Santa Spoon

Spoon up a serving of fun with this adorable Santa. It makes a great ornament or package topper!

Materials (per child)

- white plastic spoon
- cotton ball
- red felt scraps
- 2" length of white or red ribbon
- black permanent marker
- scissors
- glue

Directions

1. Cut a one-inch triangle hat from a red felt scrap.
2. Turn the spoon so the back faces up and glue the hat to the rounded end of the spoon.
3. Roll a small piece of cotton into a ball and glue it to the top of the hat.
4. Gently stretch the remaining cotton into a beard.
5. Glue the beard to the spoon as shown.
6. Cut a small mouth from red felt and glue it to the beard.
7. Use the permanent marker to draw eyes and a nose.
8. Tie the ribbon ends together.
9. Glue the knotted ends of the ribbon to the back of the hat.

Curriculum Connection
Social Studies

Have students study how Santa Claus is perceived in different cultures. Ask your students to assist you in making a chart showing similarities and differences between their Santa beliefs and the beliefs of children in other countries.

Amy Barsanti • Roper, NC

Fingerprint Wreath

Parents' faces will be wreathed in smiles when they receive this holiday memento!

Materials (per child)

- frozen-juice can lid
- white paper circle (cut to fit lid)
- green tempera paint
- red marker
- 5" length of red ribbon
- 1" self-sticking magnet strip
- glue

Directions

1. Dip your finger into the green paint.
2. Press your finger onto the outer portion of the paper circle.
3. Repeat Steps 1 and 2 until you form a wreath.
4. Use the marker to add a holiday message and red berries to the wreath.
5. Tie the ribbon into a bow.
6. Glue the bow to the bottom of the wreath.
7. Glue the paper circle to the juice lid.
8. Attach the magnet strip to the back of the lid.

Curriculum Connection
Math

Before the lesson, challenge each student to estimate how many fingerprints will fit around the edge of his paper circle. Graph the predictions. After the project, have youngsters graph how many prints actually fit. Discuss the results with the class.

Amy Barsanti • Roper, NC

Angel Puzzle Pin

Your little angels are sure to love giving these heavenly holiday pins as gifts!

Materials (per child)

- copy of the wing and dress patterns on page 83
- large puzzle piece
- colored construction paper scraps
- beads or other decorative trim
- pin back
- colored markers
- scissors
- glue

Directions

1. Trace the wing and dress patterns onto a desired color of construction paper and cut them out. (Note: The wing and dress patterns may need to be reduced or enlarged ahead of time to fit the puzzle piece.)
2. Cut a small yellow oval from the construction paper scraps for a halo.
3. Glue the dress to the unprinted side of the puzzle piece.
4. Glue the wings and halo to the printed side of the puzzle piece as shown.
5. Glue the beads or other trim to the dress.
6. Use the markers to add facial features.
7. Glue the pin back to the back of the project.

Curriculum Connection
Character Education

Pair your class with students from a younger class. Invite each child to serve as a reading "guardian angel." At a designated time, have each guardian angel read a selected book to his assigned youngster. Continue this tradition well beyond the holiday season!

Amy Barsanti • Roper, NC

Reindeer Clothespin Card

A new twist on a classic craft makes a cute card that can double as a tree trimmer!

Materials (per child)

- two 2½" flat-sided wooden clothespins
- 5" x 8" piece of blue construction paper
- white construction paper scraps
- brown tempera paint
- 2 wiggle eyes
- 3" length of white yarn
- red sequin
- paintbrush
- hole puncher
- scissors
- glue

Directions

1. Glue the clothespins together as shown to make a reindeer.
2. Paint all but the antlers of the reindeer brown. Let the paint dry.
3. Glue the wiggle eyes and the sequin (nose) to the top clothespin.
4. Fold the sheet of blue construction paper in half to form a card.
5. Cut "snow" from the white construction paper scraps and glue it to the front of the card.
6. Glue the reindeer atop the snow.
7. Hole-punch the white construction paper scraps. Glue the resulting circles around the reindeer.
8. Punch two holes at the top of the card front.
9. Thread the yarn through the holes and tie it into a bow.

Curriculum Connection
Writing
Have each child pen a holiday message inside his card. Invite him to present his reindeer notecard to a loved one.

Amy Barsanti • Roper, NC

Craft Candy Mobile

Dazzle the eyes and tickle the taste buds with this mouthwatering candy mobile!

Materials (per child)

- six 6" paper plates
- 3 sheets of plastic wrap (each 2' in length)
- variety of tempera paints
- wire clothes hanger
- 3 different lengths of yarn
- yarn scraps
- paintbrushes (one for each color paint)
- hole puncher
- glue

Directions

1. Glue the rims of two paper plates together so that the bottoms face outward. Repeat with the other four plates. Let the glue dry.
2. Paint the outsides of the plates to resemble hard candies.
3. Twist a length of plastic wrap around each candy.
4. Secure the wrap with two pieces of yarn scraps.
5. Bend the wire hanger as shown.
6. Punch a hole at the top of each candy.
7. Tie one end of a yarn length to each hole.
8. Tie the other end of each yarn length to the hanger, forming a mobile.

Curriculum Connection
Math

There are more than 2000 different types of candy made in the United States. Over half of these candy varieties contain chocolate, making it America's favorite candy flavor. Take a class-room poll to find out which candy flavors are favorites in your class-room. Have students create a graph displaying the results.

Cynthia Holcomb • Mertzon, TX

Teddy Bear Card

These huggable teddy bear cards will warm anyone's holiday!

Materials (per child)

- tagboard template of the teddy bear card pattern on page 84
- 4" x 11" piece of brown construction paper
- 6" x 9" piece of red construction paper
- markers
- scissors
- glue

Directions

1. Accordion-fold the brown construction paper to create four equal-sized sections.
2. Place the bear pattern so its arms and legs overlap the fold slightly on each side. Trace around the pattern.
3. Cut on the resulting outline to form a four-bear string.
4. Fold the red paper in half to form a card.
5. Glue the first and last bears to the inside of the card as shown.
6. Use the markers to decorate the cover of the card.
7. Sign your name on the inside of the card.

Curriculum Connection
Writing

Challenge each youngster to think of four household chores she could perform to help out at home. Have her write each chore on a different bear. Invite her to present her special gift to a loved one.

VaReane Gray Heese • Omaha, NE

Clip Mitten

These marvelous mittens will brighten any clothesline!

Materials (per child)

- tagboard template of the mitten patterns on page 84
- two 6" squares of different felt colors
- assorted buttons and sequins
- fabric paints
- snap-closure hair clip
- scissors
- craft glue
- marker (for tracing patterns)

Directions

1. Trace each mitten pattern onto a different color of felt.
2. Cut out the patterns.
3. Glue the smaller mitten shape atop the larger one.
4. Use the fabric paints to decorate the mitten as desired.
5. Glue the buttons and sequins to the mitten.
6. Glue the hair clip to the back of the project as shown.
7. Display the colorful mittens by snapping them onto a stretched length of yarn.

Curriculum Connection
Math and Language Arts

Ask students to name other objects that come in pairs. List their responses on the chalkboard. Challenge each child to write a story problem about a pair of objects. Staple two lengths of yarn to a large bulletin board. Clip the story problems to the line. Display the clip mittens near the story problems.

VaReane Gray Heese • Omaha, NE

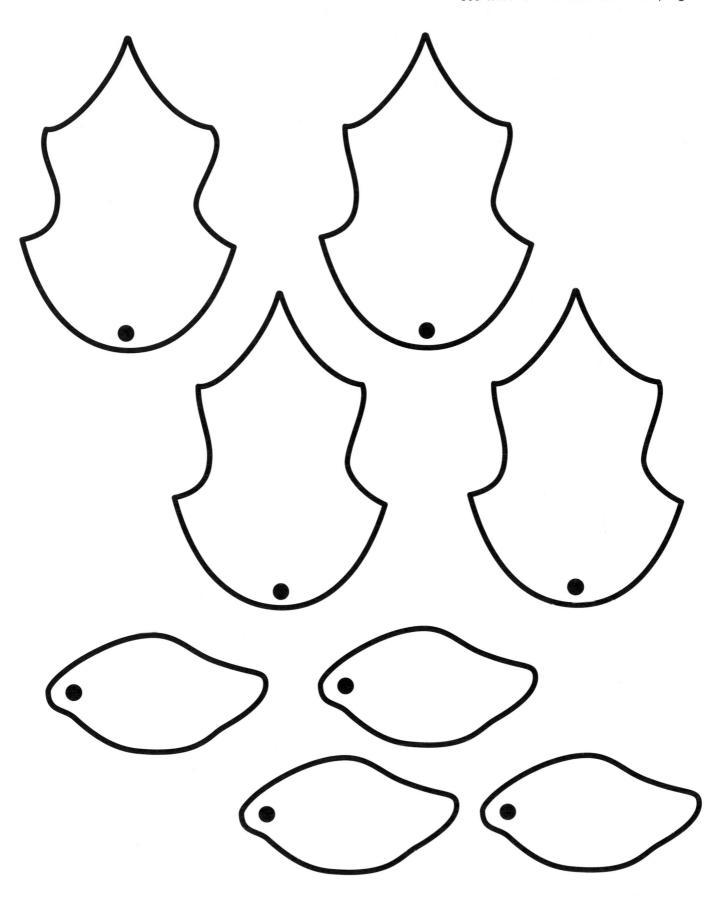

Christmas Flower Leaf Patterns
Use with "Christmas Flower" on page 72.

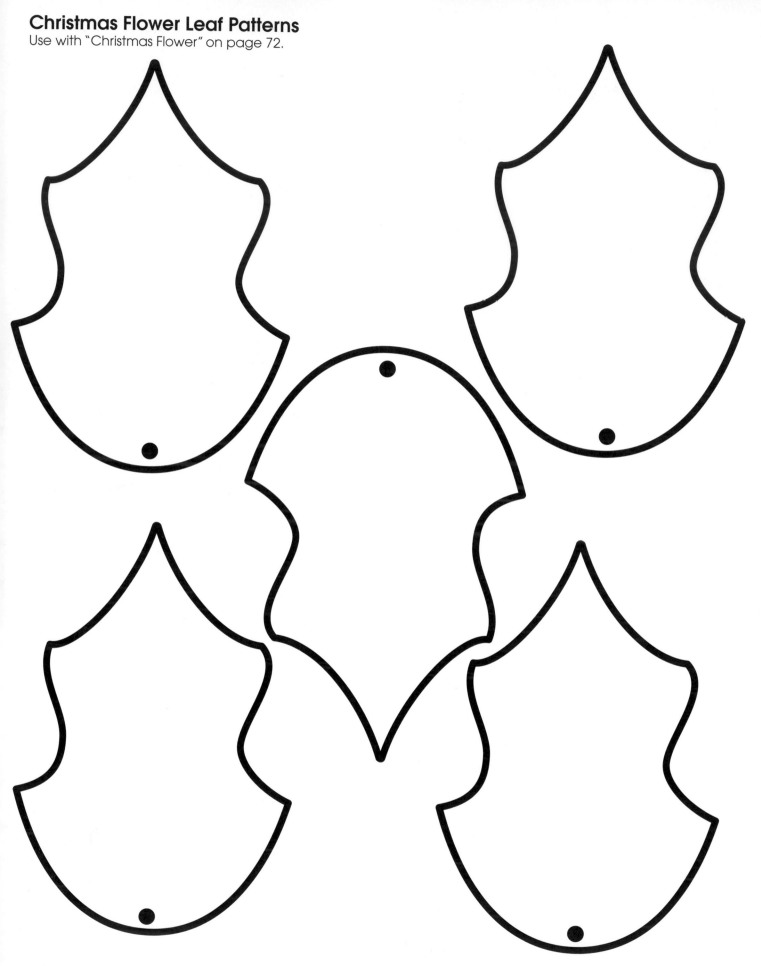

Teddy Bear Card Patterns
Use with "Teddy Bear Card" on page 79.

Mitten Patterns
Use with "Clip Mitten" on page 80.

JANUARY

New Year's Bell

Ring in the New Year with these three-dimensional mobiles!

Materials (per child)

- 9" x 12" sheet of colored construction paper
- copy of the bell pattern on page 97
- paper clip
- scissors
- fishing line
- hole puncher

Directions

1. Cut out the bell pattern along the outer edge only.
2. Fold the sheet of construction paper in half.
3. Lay the dotted-line edge of the pattern along the construction paper fold, and paper-clip in place.
4. Beginning at A, carefully cut through the construction paper along the bell outline.
5. Next, cut along the solid line beginning at B. Stop where indicated.
6. Then cut along the solid line beginning at C. Stop where indicated.
7. Remove the pattern and open the bell.
8. Fold the center section back slightly.
9. Punch a hole at the top of the bell.
10. Use the fishing line to create a hanger.

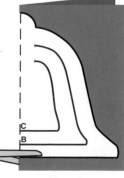

Step 4

Curriculum Connection
Language Arts

Ask each child to share his New Year's resolution. Have him write his resolution on a 3" x 5" card. Direct the youngster to tape his card to an additional length of fishing line; then have him tape the line to the bottom of his bell. Suspend the mobiles around the room for everyone to enjoy.

VaReane Gray Heese • Omaha, NE

Blizzard Snowman

Create a blizzard of fun in your classroom with this snowman project!

Materials (per child)

- white and colored construction paper scraps
- 9" x 12" sheet of blue construction paper
- shallow box or box lid at least 9" x 12"
- spoon
- small bowl
- white tempera paint
- marble
- glue

Directions

1. Tear the construction paper scraps to make a snowman, and glue it in the middle of the sheet of blue construction paper.
2. Place the project in the box.
3. Pour a small amount of paint into the bowl and put in the marble.
4. Carefully lift the marble out with the spoon and place it atop the project.
5. Lift the box and gently roll the marble around the paper. Repeat to create a desired blizzard effect.

Curriculum Connection
Language Arts

Have each child write a story about the day his snowman got lost in a blizzard. Staple his story to the bottom of his paper. Display the projects around the room for a blizzard of reading fun!

Candi Deal • Dalton, GA

Sparkling Snowflake

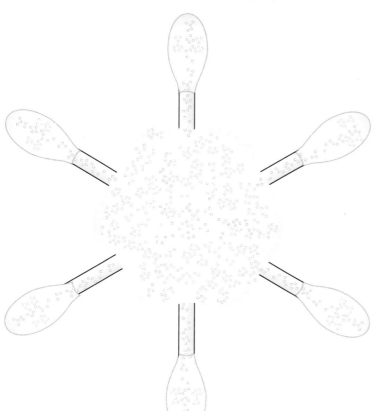

These snowflakes are sure to add a sparkle to your classroom.

Materials (per child)

- square of waxed paper
- 3 cotton swabs (cut in half)
- cotton ball
- glue
- glitter

Directions

1. Lay the waxed paper over the workspace.
2. Lay the cotton swabs on the waxed paper to form a snowflake as shown.
3. Apply a generous amount of glue where the ends meet and place a cotton ball atop the glue. Let the glue dry.
4. Put glue along each cotton swab and on the middle of the cotton ball.
5. Sprinkle glitter over the glue and shake off the excess.
6. When the project is completely dry, carefully peel it from the waxed paper.

Curriculum Connection Math

Invite your youngsters to explore symmetry with snowflakes. Have each child fold a sheet of blue construction paper in half lengthwise. Have him paint one half of a snowflake near the fold on one side of his paper. Direct him to fold his paper together, gently pressing the two sides together. Then have him unfold his paper and describe the symmetry of his snowflake.

Amy Barsanti • Roper, NC

Sock Snowbaby

The weather outside may be frightful—but these snowbabies sure are delightful!

Materials (per child)

- white baby sock
- facial tissues
- two 2" lengths of brown pipe cleaner
- ³⁄₈" piece of orange pipe cleaner
- narrow ribbon
- thread or string
- glue
- black permanent marker

Directions

1. Stuff two or three tissues inside the sock, leaving approximately two inches unstuffed.
2. Tie the sock off with a length of thread.
3. Fold the top of the sock down to form a hat.
4. Tie a length of ribbon near the middle of the snowbaby, creating a scarf, head, and body.
5. Bend the brown pipe cleaner lengths to make twig arms.
6. Push the arms into the sides of the snowbaby and secure them with glue.
7. Push the orange pipe cleaner (the nose) into the head of the snowbaby and secure it with glue.
8. Use the marker to add snowbaby features to the project.

Curriculum Connection
Language Arts

When each child has completed his project, share with your students Raymond Briggs's wordless picture book, *The Snowman*. After discussing the story, invite each child to create his own wordless picture book about his snowbaby.

Amy Barsanti • Roper, NC

Totally Tubular Penguin

These penguins are totally tubular!

Materials (per child)

- 7" x 2½" strip of black construction paper
- 2½" length of paper towel tubing
- black, orange, and white construction paper scraps
- 2 wiggle eyes
- scissors
- glue

Directions

1. Glue the black construction paper strip around the paper towel tube.
2. Cut a small white construction paper oval (belly) and glue it to the tube (penguin).
3. Cut a small orange construction paper triangle (beak) and glue it above the belly.
4. Cut two small black construction paper wings and glue them on either side of the penguin.
5. Glue the wiggle eyes above the beak.

Curriculum Connection
Science

Have small groups of students investigate penguins. Then have each group act out scenes from a penguin's day based on the research findings.

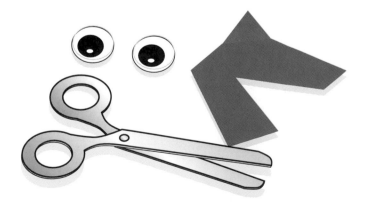

Becky Shelley • Grove, OK

Polar Bear Puppet

Your youngsters are sure to love these polar puppet pals!

Materials (per child)

- white lunch sack
- 1" square of black construction paper
- 1" x 2" piece of blue construction paper
- scissors
- glue

Directions

1. With the flap (bag's bottom) facing up, fold under the lower points as shown.
2. Cut an oval (nose) from the black construction paper.
3. Glue the nose to the lower edge of the flap.
4. Cut two circles from the blue construction paper and glue them to the bag for eyes.
5. Trim about two inches from the bottom of the puppet (opening of the bag).
6. Cut two circular ears from the bag trimmings; glue them to the top of the puppet.

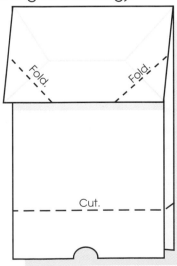

Fold   Fold

Cut.

Curriculum Connection
Science

Polar bears have fur on the soles of their feet. The fur helps their feet stay warm and keeps them from slipping on ice. Ask student pairs to research one additional fact about polar bears. Have each pair present its fact to the class with the aid of their polar puppets.

VaReane Gray Heese • Omaha, NE

Walrus Wonderland

Create a walrus wonderland in your classroom with this painting project!

Materials (per child)

white construction paper copy of
    the walrus pattern on page 98
9" x 12" sheet of white construction
    paper
12" x 18" sheet of blue construction
    paper
4–6 cotton balls
blue and purple watercolor paints
brown tempera paint
small piece of sponge
small bowl of water
large paintbrush
scissors
glue

Directions

1. Paint the white sheet of construction paper with blue and purple water-colors. (Dip the brush into the water frequently to create a washed look.) Let the paint dry completely.
2. Glue the painted paper to the large sheet of blue construction paper, creating a frame for the painting.
3. Pull apart the cotton balls. Glue them to the bottom of the picture for snow.
4. Sponge-paint the walrus pattern with brown tempera paint. Let the walrus dry; then cut the pattern out.
5. Glue the walrus cutout to the project atop the snow.

Curriculum Connection
Writing

Ask students to brainstorm what a walrus uses its tusks for (climbing on the ice, stirring up clams, and fighting). Have each child write a list of ten ways he'd use his tusks if he were a walrus. Display the lists near the projects.

Darcy Brown

We Are Alike

This class bookmaking project will encourage your students to cherish differences and look for similarities among their classmates.

Materials (per child)

- copy of the body pattern on page 99
- copy of the poem on page 99
- 9" x 6" piece of colored construction paper
- crayons or markers
- scissors
- glue

Directions

1. On the pattern, write one thing that most humans have in common. (*Discuss this in advance to get a variety of responses. If desired, write the ideas on a chalkboard for students to refer to.*)
2. Decorate the body pattern to resemble yourself.
3. Cut out the shape.
4. Glue the shape to the construction paper.
5. Give your project to your teacher to include in a class book. (*See Curriculum Connection.*)

Cindy Barber • Fredonia, WI

Curriculum Connection

Reading

Create this class book in a few simple steps; then share it with your students for a take-home reading opportunity. To make a book, punch holes two inches from the top and bottom on the right and left sides of each child's project. Attach paper reinforcers; then use small pieces of yarn to connect the projects. Create a title page using the poem on page 99. Attach it to the student projects. Then accordion-fold the set to create a book.

Dream Pendant

These unique necklaces will remind your youngsters of Martin Luther King Jr.'s dream of peace.

Materials (per child)

- white construction paper copy of the patterns on page 100
- 18" length of yarn
- crayons
- pencil
- scissors
- glue

Directions

1. Color the pattern with King's picture; then cut the patterns out.
2. Write about a dream of peace on each cloud pattern.
3. Lay the yarn out straight.
4. Fold each pattern along the dotted line.
5. Glue the inside of each pattern shape together around the yarn as shown.
6. Tie the yarn ends together.

Curriculum Connection
Social Studies

Invite your students' families in for a "Dream of Peace" tea. Provide fruit punch and cookies. Have each youngster read aloud his dreams of peace from his pendant to the visitors. If desired, ask parent volunteers to share their own dreams of peace.

Darcy Brown

"Dino-mite" Gift Bag

Turn a simple lunch sack into a "dino-mite" gift bag in a snap!

Materials (per child)

- lunch sack
- dinosaur stencils or patterns
- patterned wrapping paper or fabric scraps
- length of twine
- pencil
- scissors
- glue
- hole puncher

Directions

1. With the opening of the sack facing up, trace a stencil onto one side of the sack.
2. Cut out the dinosaur shape from the sack.
3. Cut a square of wrapping paper and glue it inside the bag to cover the opening.
4. Cut an additional piece of wrapping paper for a gift tag. Punch a hole in the tag.
5. Fold the top of the bag down approximately two inches.
6. Punch two holes, one on each side of the top of the folded bag.
7. Thread the length of twine through the holes and through the gift tag. Tie the ends into a bow.

Curriculum Connection
Social Studies

Before tying the bag closed, invite each child to make a special gift or treat. Have each child place his gift into his bag and tie it closed. Ask him to present his gift to a loved one.

VaReane Gray Heese • Omaha, NE

"Thar" She Blows!

This winsome whale is sure to make a splash with your students!

Materials (per child)

- white paper lunch sack
- shallow bowl of blue tempera paint
- cotton ball
- clothespin
- coffee filter
- rubber band
- construction paper scraps
- newspaper
- scissors
- glue

Directions

1. With the bag flat, cut a triangle from the open end as shown.
2. Clip the cotton ball to the clothespin.
3. Dip the cotton ball into the paint. Use the cotton to sponge-paint the entire bag. Let the paint dry.
4. Stuff the sack half full of newspaper to make a whale.
5. Twist the open end of the bag and secure it with the rubber band to form the tail.
6. Fold the coffee filter into fourths. Twist the bottom of the folded filter.
7. Turn the bag on its side and cut a small slit in the top. Slip the twisted end of the filter through the slit and glue it in place.
8. Cut out construction paper eyes and a mouth and glue them to the whale.

Curriculum Connection
Science

Whales are animals who travel in groups called pods. Have your children research other names for different groups of animals. Display the findings near the whale projects.

Cynthia Holcomb • Mertzon, TX

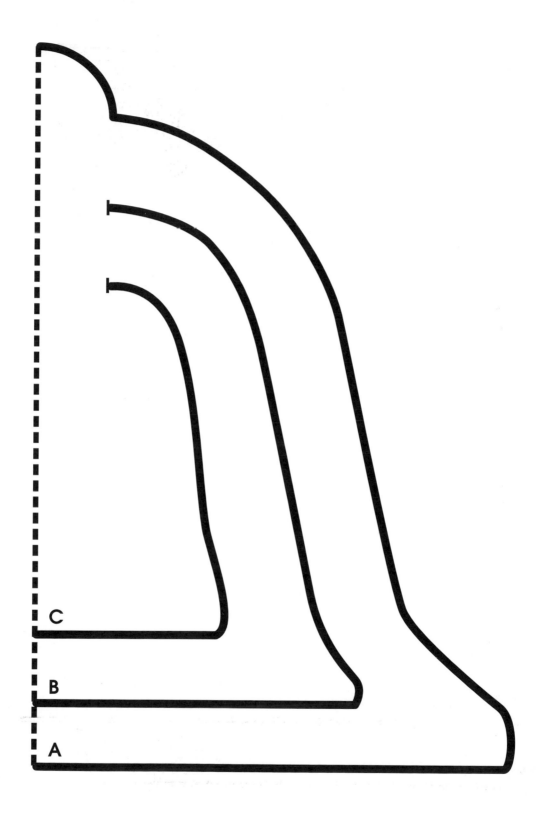

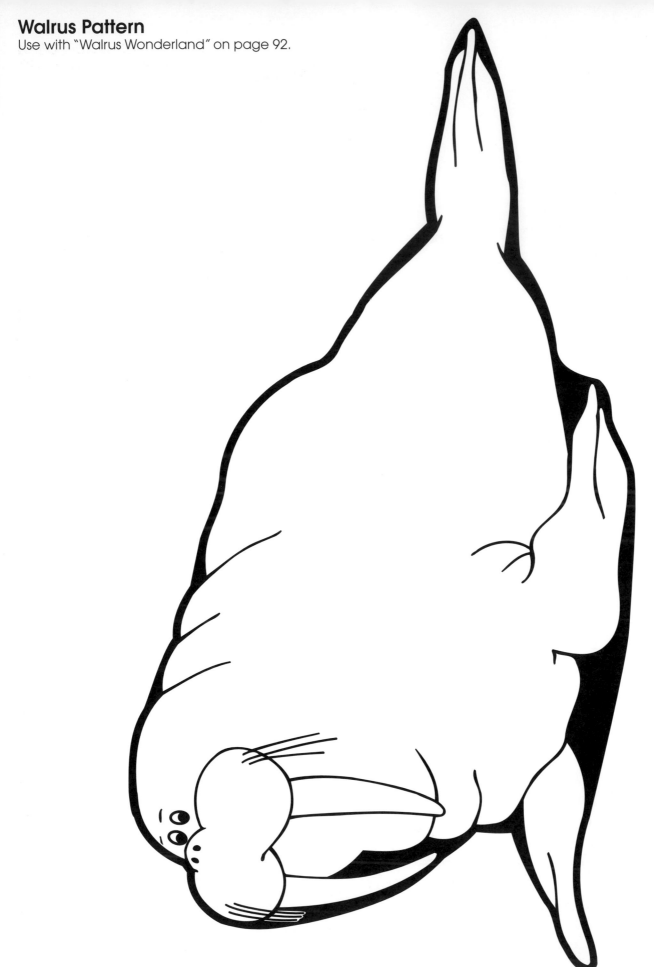

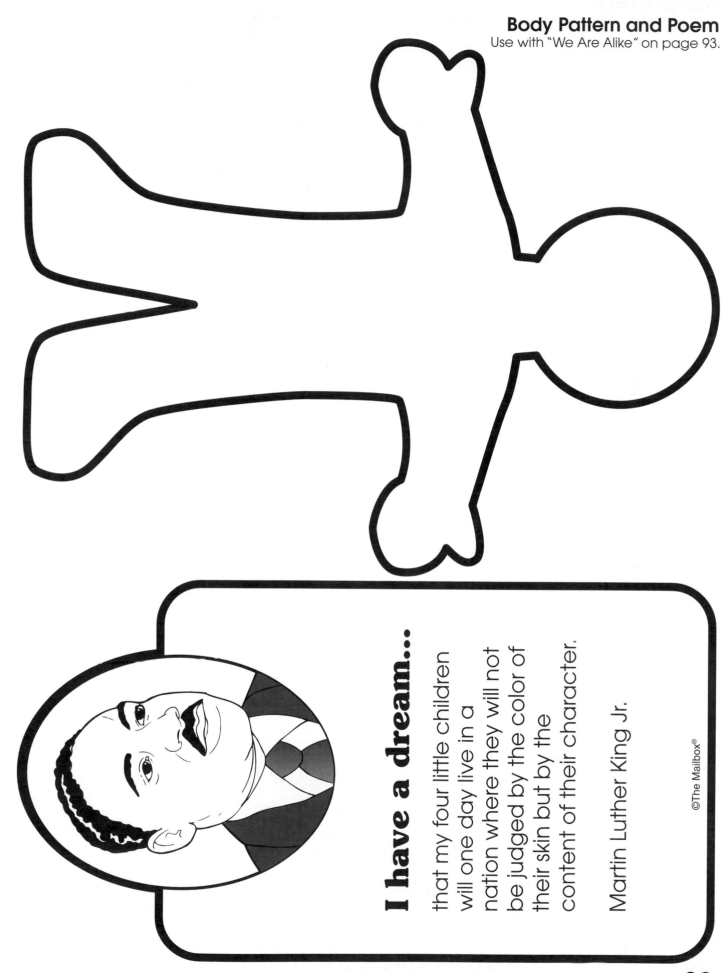

I have a dream...

that my four little children
will one day live in a
nation where they will not
be judged by the color of
their skin but by the
content of their character.

Martin Luther King Jr.

©The Mailbox®

Dream Pendant Patterns

Use with "Dream Pendant" on page 94.

FEBRUARY

Groundhog Shadow Puppet

It's Groundhog Day! Will there be six more weeks of winter, or is spring just around the corner?

Materials (per child)

tagboard copy of the groundhog shadow pattern on page 117
5" square of brown cardboard
5" square of black poster board
craft stick
black fine-tip marker
pencil
scissors
glue

Directions

1. Cut out the groundhog pattern.
2. Trace the pattern onto the cardboard square. Trace the pattern onto the black poster board square. Cut out both shapes.
3. Draw groundhog features on the front of the cardboard shape with the marker.
4. Fold back the tab on each pattern.
5. Glue the groundhog and its shadow to opposite ends of the craft stick as shown.

Curriculum Connection
Science

Invite your students to experiment with shadows. On a sunny day, have your students stand outdoors with their backs to the sun. Ask each child to describe what he sees. Ask volunteers to explain why they think shadows appear.

Amy Barsanti • Roper, NC

Groundhog Poster

This poster is sure to remind your youngsters what happens when the groundhog sees his shadow!

Materials (per child)

- copy of the groundhog poems on page 117
- light-brown construction paper copy of the groundhog pattern on page 118
- 12" x 18" sheet of white paper
- 2" x 9" piece of brown paper
- 2" x 6" piece of black paper
- 9" x 12" piece of blue paper
- 4" x 9" piece of green paper
- construction paper scraps
- crayons
- scissors
- glue

Directions

1. Fold the white paper in half. Unfold the paper.
2. Trim the blue paper to resemble a winter sky. Glue the sky to the top right side of the white paper.
3. Cut the green paper to resemble grass. Glue it to the bottom left side of the white paper.
4. Cut the black paper into an oval for a shadow. Glue it to the bottom right side of the paper.
5. Cut out the groundhog pattern. Glue it to the middle of the white paper.
6. Trim the brown construction paper to resemble a mound of dirt. Glue it to the white paper as shown.
7. Add additional spring and winter decorations as desired.
8. Cut out the groundhog poems. Glue each poem to the correct side of the paper.

Curriculum Connection
Science

Invite your youngsters to compare spring to winter using a Venn diagram. After completing the diagram as a class, have each child draw a picture to accompany the chart.

Cindy Barber • Fredonia, WI

Chinese New Year Lantern

These Chinese New Year lanterns are sure to have your youngsters shouting, "Gung Hay Fat Choy!" (Happy New Year!)

Materials (per child)

- two 14 oz. foam cups
- 10" length of yarn
- sharpened pencil
- seven ½" x 8" colored construction paper strips
- craft glue
- colored permanent markers
- large sequins

Directions

1. Use the pencil to poke two holes in the bottom of one cup.
2. Thread the yarn through the holes and tie the yarn ends together to form a hanger.
3. Accordion-fold the strips of construction paper.
4. Glue the strips to the bottom of the other cup.
5. Glue the two cups together as shown.
6. Decorate the lantern with markers.
7. Glue the sequins to the lantern as desired.

Curriculum Connection
Social Studies

Traditionally, Chinese New Year festivities culminate with a lantern parade to light the way for the new year. Have one or two students tell other classes about this tradition through a brief oral presentation; then have your students join together carrying their lanterns to form a lantern parade through neighboring classrooms.

Darcy Brown

Patriotic Centerpiece

Show your patriotism by creating a symbolic centerpiece for your family to use on Presidents' Day!

Materials (per child)

- 3 tubes of various sizes (such as a paper towel tube, toilet tissue tube, and potato chip canister)
- 9" x 12" sheet each of red, white, and blue construction paper
- 2" star-shaped template
- patriotic stickers (optional)
- scissors
- glue

Directions

1. If necessary, trim the tops off one or more tubes so that they are different lengths.
2. Glue one sheet of construction paper around each tube and trim the edges of the paper. Save the paper scraps.
3. Cut stars (using the template) and stripes from the scraps of construction paper.
4. Glue the stars and stripes to the tubes as desired.
5. Apply the stickers to the tubes if desired.
6. Glue the tubes together and place the arrangement on a table.

Curriculum Connection
Social Studies

Have small groups of students research the meanings for the colors of the U.S. flag. Challenge each group to dramatically present its findings to the class.

VaReane Gray Heese • Omaha, NE

Lean Lincoln

Your youngsters will love to set this project out for others to admire!

Materials (per child)

- paper towel tube
- 7 ½" x 6" piece of black paper
- 2" x 6" strip of manila paper
- 2" x 6" strip of black paper
- 3" circle of black paper
- two 8 ½" x 1" strips of black paper
- two 5" x ½" strips of black paper
- markers
- glue
- 3 small white buttons
- scissors

Directions

1. Glue the large black sheet of paper around the tube to cover 7 ½ inches beginning at one end.
2. Glue the manila strip of paper around the tube, overlapping the existing black piece slightly.
3. Glue the 2" x 6" strip of black paper around the tube, overlapping the manila paper slightly and covering the tube to the end.
4. Center the end of the tube atop the black paper circle and trace the tube's end.
5. Cut along the tracing and then slip the ring over the end of the tube. Glue in place as shown to form a hat rim.
6. Glue the shorter black strips to either side of the body for arms.
7. Glue the longer black strips inside the tube's end (opposite the hat) for legs.
8. Draw facial features using the markers.
9. Glue the buttons to the coat.

VaReane Gray Heese • Omaha, NE

Curriculum Connection
Social Studies

Abraham Lincoln was affectionately known as "Honest Abe." After discussing the meaning of honesty with your students, have each child act out a situation in which he made an honest decision.

By George...It's George!

Add more smiles to your classroom with these famous faces.

Materials (per child)

- paper plate
- flesh-toned tempera paint
- 12" x 3" piece of blue construction paper
- red and black construction paper scraps
- 8 cotton balls
- paintbrush
- scissors
- glue
- markers

Directions

1. Paint the plate with flesh-toned paint. Let the paint dry.
2. Fold the plate in half with the paint to the outside.
3. Trim the blue paper as shown.
4. Glue the paper to the folded edge of the plate.
5. Glue four cotton balls on either side of the plate to create a wig.
6. Cut facial features from the construction paper scraps and glue them to the plate.
7. Add additional features with a marker.

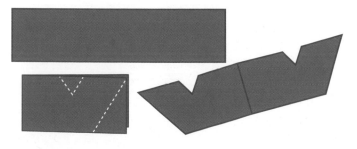

Curriculum Connection
Writing

Provide students with a variety of facts or quotes related to George Washington. Have each child write a selected statement about George Washington on the inside of his folded plate. Staple the completed projects to a bulletin board titled "By George...It's George!"

Darcy Brown

Lovebird

This lovebird pin makes a great Valentine's Day gift!

Materials (per child)

- red craft feather
- 1" red pom-pom
- ½" red pom-pom
- 2 small wiggle eyes
- pin back
- scrap of orange construction paper
- scissors
- craft glue

Directions

1. Glue the larger pom-pom near the base of the feather, and glue the smaller pom-pom to the feather atop the larger pom-pom.
2. Glue the wiggle eyes to the small pom-pom.
3. Cut a small beak from the orange construction paper scrap.
4. Glue the beak beneath the eyes.
5. Let the project dry completely.
6. Glue the pin back to the back of the project.

Curriculum Connection
Math

Before giving these lovely love-birds as gifts, use the class set to model subtraction problems. Show the birds "flying away" as each problem is being solved.

Amy Barsanti • Roper, NC

"Mappy" Valentine's Day!

You'll find your way to your students' hearts with these happy, "mappy" valentines!

Materials (per child)

- 6" x 9" piece of construction paper
- 4" square cut from an old map
- scissors
- markers
- glue

Directions

1. Fold the piece of construction paper in half to form a card.
2. Cut a heart from the map square and glue it to the front of the card.
3. On the front of the card, write "You found the way…"
4. On the inside of the card, write the caption "…to my heart. Happy Valentine's Day!"
5. Write a closing and signature at the bottom of the card.

my heart.

Happy Valentine's Day

Love, Amy

You found the way…

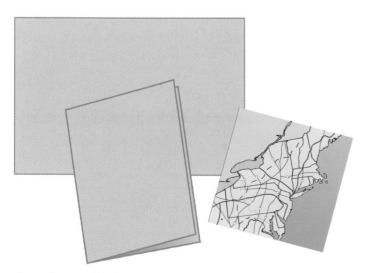

Curriculum Connection
Creative Writing

Challenge your youngsters to brainstorm additional "mappy" phrases, like "A Compass Rose for My Love!" and "From East to West… You're the Best!" Invite students to make additional valentines to share with their loved ones.

Amy Barsanti • Roper, NC

Rebus Valentine

These rebus valentines will add some spunk to your Valentine's Day fun!

Materials (per child)

- red construction paper copy of the rectangle pattern on page 119
- pink construction paper copy of the heart pattern on page 119
- construction paper scraps
- old magazine, newspaper, or grocery store circular
- markers
- scissors
- glue

Directions

1. Cut out the heart and rectangle patterns.
2. Glue the heart to the rectangle.
3. Cut magazine or circular pictures to create a rebus message.
4. Write and glue the message on the heart shape.
5. Cut small hearts or other decorations from the construction paper scraps and glue them to the valentine.

Curriculum Connection
Language Arts

Before students create their rebus valentines, brainstorm several rebus phrases as a class. Write the students' responses on a sheet of chart paper. Direct students to refer to the list of phrases as they create their rebus valentines.

VaReane Gray Heese • Omaha, NE

Flavorful Freight Engine

These tasty treats are as sweet as they look!

Materials (per child)

- roll Life Savers candy
- five-piece pack of gum
- wrapped Rolo candy
- 2 Starburst candies
- Hershey's Kisses candy
- 4 round, wrapped hard candies
- craft glue

Directions

1. Glue the Life Savers roll to the wide, flat side of the pack of gum. (Let the glue dry completely after each step.)
2. Glue the Rolo candy to one end of the Life Savers roll.
3. Glue the four round candies to the sides of the gum pack to make wheels.
4. Glue the Hershey's Kisses candy to the top of the Life Savers roll near the end with the Rolo forming a smokestack.
5. Glue the two Starburst candies together atop the Life Savers roll (opposite the smokestack).

Curriculum Connection
Social Studies

Have youngsters investigate different types of transportation. Instruct each child to cut magazine pictures of various modes of transportation. Challenge her to create a timeline showing the history of her transportation types.

VaReane Gray Heese • Omaha, NE

Goldilocks and the Three Bears

These nifty nesting cups are sure to bring a favorite fairy tale to life!

Materials (per child)

- two 3 oz. paper cups
- 5 oz. paper cup
- 7 oz. paper cup
- 9" x 12" sheet of brown construction paper
- 6" x 9" sheet of manila construction paper
- construction paper scraps
- scissors
- glue
- markers

Directions

1. Glue brown construction paper around one of the three-ounce cups. Trim the paper to fit. Repeat with the five- and seven-ounce cups.
2. Glue the manila construction paper around the other three-ounce cup. Trim the paper to fit.
3. Invert each of the cups.
4. Cut bear features, such as ears and other identifying characteristics, from the construction paper scraps and glue them to each brown cup to make Papa, Mama, and Baby Bear.
5. Cut Goldilocks' hair and facial features from the construction paper scraps and glue them to the remaining cup.
6. Use markers to add additional facial features.

Curriculum Connection
Language Arts

Read aloud your favorite version of Goldilocks and the Three Bears. Have each youngster retell the story using her nesting cups.

Mary Rosenberg • Fresno, CA

Candy House

Nibble, nibble, like a mouse…who's that nibbling at my house? Could it be Hansel and Gretel?

Materials (per child)

- brown paper lunch sack
- crumpled scrap paper
- 5" x 6" piece of brown paper
- 2" x 4" piece of red paper
- brown and red paper scraps
- white tagboard copy of the character patterns on page 120
- fabric paint pens and/or small candies in a variety of colors
- cotton ball
- crayons
- access to a stapler
- glue
- scissors

Directions

1. Fill the sack half-full with the crumpled scrap paper. Fold the top of the sack down and staple it.
2. Fold the brown paper in half. Trim the open edges to resemble shingles.
3. Glue the paper atop the bag to make a roof.
4. Fold the red piece of paper in half and cut a slit in the fold.
5. Pull the cotton ball gently apart and push it partway through the slit, making a chimney and smoke.
6. Glue the chimney atop the roof.
7. Cut house details from the paper scraps and glue them to the house.
8. Decorate the house with the fabric paints and candy.
9. Color, cut out, and assemble the character patterns.
10. Place the characters around the completed house.

Cynthia Holcomb • Mertzon, TX

Curriculum Connection
Language Arts

Retell your favorite version of *Hansel and Gretel*. Have students describe the *beginning* and *middle* of the story. Challenge them to rewrite the *end* of the story in their own words.

Cereal Box Castle

No fairy tale would be complete without a majestic castle. This one is so simple to make, you'll have a kingdom in your classroom in no time!

Materials (per child)

- empty cereal box
- 9" piece of black yarn or cord
- black permanent marker
- hole puncher
- clear tape
- scissors

Directions

1. Open the flaps at the top and bottom of the box.
2. Cut along one corner of the cereal box.
3. Lay the box flat, gray side up.
4. Trim the flaps off the bottom of the box.
5. Cut a door at the bottom of one of the large panels.
6. Trim the top flaps of the box to resemble a castle.
7. Use the marker to draw window and door details and bricks.
8. Punch a hole through the door and the adjacent side panel as shown.
9. Thread the yarn through the hole in the panel and knot at the end.
10. Thread the yarn through the hole in the door and secure it to the back with tape.
11. Refold the box, inside out, and tape the cut edges of the castle together.

Curriculum Connection
Social Studies

Display the castles on a countertop in the classroom. Have small groups of students research life in medieval times. Challenge each group to create construction paper characters to display near the castles.

Patti Moeser • McFarland, WI

Dental Delight

Help your students brush up on their dental health habits with this cute craft!

Materials (per child)

- 6" x 18" piece of colored tagboard
- 3" x 6" piece of white felt
- markers
- scissors
- glue

Directions

1. Cut a 12" x 3" piece from the tagboard, as shown, leaving a toothbrush shape.
2. Make cuts about three-fourths inch apart along one long side of the felt piece, stopping each cut about one inch from the opposite side.
3. Draw a line of glue along the uncut side of the felt.
4. Glue the felt onto the toothbrush as shown.
5. Write your name on the toothbrush above the felt piece.

Brush, brush, brush your teeth;
Brush them twice a day.
Up, down, all around,
So germs will go away!

Curriculum Connection
Writing

Have each youngster copy the following poem onto an index card. Then have him glue the poem on the handle of his toothbrush.

Brush, brush, brush your teeth;
Brush them twice a day.
Up, down, all around,
So germs will go away!

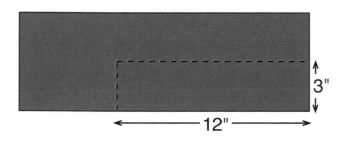

3"

12"

Darcy Brown

Forever Friends Necklaces

Celebrate International Friendship Week (held the last week of February) with these one-of-a-kind necklaces!

Materials (per child)

- air-dry or wet-set clay
- markers
- plastic knife
- 2 metal *U* shapes (such as an end cut from a paper clip)
- six 24" lengths of embroidery floss or string in different colors
- pencil
- masking tape
- ruler

Directions

1. Roll the clay into a 1½-inch ball. Press the ball flat to about ⅛-inch thickness.
2. Draw a heart on the flattened clay. Cut the heart out with the knife.
3. Cut the heart into two pieces as shown.
4. Push a metal *U* into the top of each heart piece. Let air-dry.
5. Tie the ends of three strands of floss together.
6. Tape the knotted ends to a desk.
7. Braid the lengths together, stopping about one inch from the end. Remove the tape and knot the ends.
8. Repeat Steps 5–7 using the remaining three strands of floss.
9. Decorate the dried clay pieces with markers.
10. Thread half a heart onto each braid.
11. Knot the ends of each braid necklace together.

Curriculum Connection
Social Studies

Set aside time during International Friendship Week for a necklace exchange party. Have pairs of students give one another one of their necklaces. After the exchange, invite each child to say something special about her friend.

Amy Barsanti • Roper, NC
VaReane Gray Heese • Omaha, NE

Groundhog Poems
Use with "Groundhog Poster" on page 103.

I look outside;
My shadow I see.
It's six more weeks of winter for me!

I peek outside and see wonderful things.
I think I'll come out
And welcome spring!

Groundhog Pattern
Use with "Groundhog Poster" on page 103.

Rectangle and Heart Pattern

Use the rectangle pattern and the heart pattern with "Rebus Valentine" on page 110.

Character and Stand Patterns
Use with "Candy House" on page 113.

Gretel

Hansel

Old Woman

Directions:
1. Cut each piece along the heavy outline and the dotted line.
2. Slide the bottom of the character pattern down into the slit as shown.

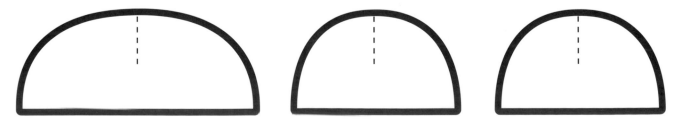

MARCH

"Roarrring" Magnets

Let these "roarrring" lion magnets keep watch over your youngsters' important papers!

Materials (per child)

- 6–10 discarded puzzle pieces
- frozen-juice lid
- 2" strip of magnetic tape
- 2 wiggle eyes
- light brown tempera paint
- 3" square of yellow construction paper
- black fine-tip permanent marker
- pencil
- paintbrush
- craft glue
- scissors

Directions

1. Paint the cardboard side of the puzzle pieces light brown. Let the paint dry.
2. Trace the juice lid onto the yellow construction paper and cut out the circle.
3. Draw a lion face on the circle with the marker.
4. Glue the wiggle eyes in place on the lion face.
5. Glue the puzzle pieces, painted side up, around the edges of the juice lid.
6. Glue the lion face atop the center of the juice lid. Let the glue dry completely.
7. Apply the magnetic tape to the back of the project.

Curriculum Connection
Science

Have each youngster investigate lions. Provide a variety of research materials for students. Challenge each child to write about a lion's animal group, characteristics, and eating habits. Set aside time for each child to share her findings with her classmates.

Colleen Dabney • Williamsburg, VA

Lion Doorknob Decor

Your youngsters are sure to love these cute doorknob displays!

Materials (per child)

- coffee filter
- brown tempera paint
- paintbrush
- 2 small black buttons
- pink and black craft foam
- scissors
- glue

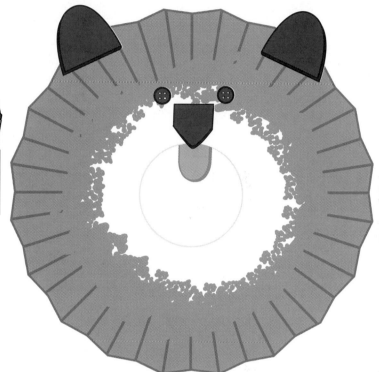

Directions

1. Fold the coffee filter in half.
2. Cut a 1½" diameter semicircle from the center of the filter.
3. Unfold the filter and paint the outer edge brown. Let the paint dry.
4. Glue the button eyes to the front of the filter.
5. Cut out a black foam nose, two black foam ears, and a pink foam tongue. Glue them to the filter.

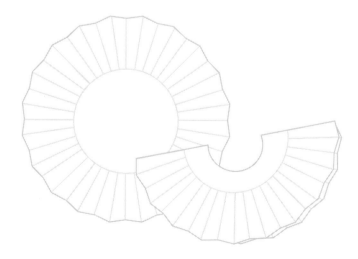

Curriculum Connection
Art

Have each child make a lamb doorknob hanger to accompany his lion. Direct each youngster to repeat Steps 1 and 2 with another filter. Have him glue cotton balls around the filter. Then direct him to glue on two button eyes, two black foam ears, a black foam nose, and a pink foam tongue to complete the project.

Colleen Dabney • Williamsburg, VA

Little Lambs

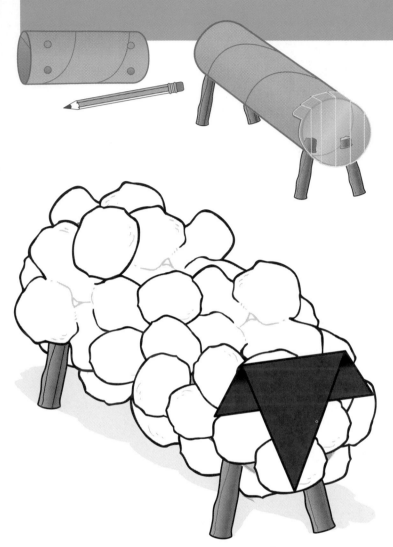

Create a whole flock in your classroom with these adorable little lambs!

Materials (per child)

- 4½" cardboard tube
- four 2" twigs, approximately the same diameter as a pencil
- cotton balls
- sharpened pencil
- black construction paper scraps
- scissors
- glue
- masking tape

Directions

1. Use the pencil to poke four leg holes in the tube as shown.
2. Push one end of each twig length into a different hole and glue in place. Let dry.
3. Seal each end of the tube with tape.
4. Glue on cotton balls to completely cover the tube.
5. Cut a two-inch equilateral triangle from the black construction paper. Fold one edge under to form a head and ears. Then glue the head to one end of the tube as shown.

Curriculum Connection
Language Arts

Challenge each child to write a poem about lambs. Direct each youngster to cut an eight-inch circle from green construction paper. Around the edges of the circle, have her write words or phrases that describe a lamb. Display each poem on a table with the child's lamb standing in the center.

Linda Masternak Justice • Kansas City, MO

Shamrock Man

This festive little shamrock man is as much fun to make as he is to look at!

Materials (per child)

- copy of the shamrock man patterns on page 134
- 9" x 12" sheet of green construction paper
- four 1" x 12" strips of green construction paper
- black construction paper
- pencil
- markers
- glue
- scissors

Directions

1. Cut out the shamrock patterns and trace one large and four small shamrocks onto the green paper. Cut out the shamrocks.
2. Accordion-fold the strips of green paper. Glue the strips to the large shamrock to create arms and legs.
3. Glue one small shamrock to the end of each arm and leg.
4. Cut out the hat pattern and trace it onto the black construction paper. Cut out the hat.
5. Glue the hat to the large shamrock as shown.
6. Draw facial features on the shamrock man.

Curriculum Connection
Math
Duplicate the small shamrock pattern to make a class supply. Place the shamrocks and pre-programmed word problem cards at a center. Have a child visit the center and use the shamrocks to solve the word problems.

Lisa Buchholz • Glen Ellyn, IL

Lucky Leprechaun

This legendary lad may not lead you to his pot of gold, but he might just bring loads of luck!

Materials (per child)

- wooden ball clothespin
- green construction paper scraps
- green pipe cleaner
- scissors
- glue
- fine-tip permanent markers
- pin back
- hot glue gun (teacher use only)

Directions

1. Cut construction paper clothes from the green scraps.
2. Glue the clothes to the clothespin.
3. Bend the pipe cleaner into a shamrock shape.
4. Glue the end of the shamrock to one sleeve.
5. Draw other features (buttons, face, hat detail) with markers.
6. Use hot glue to attach the pin back to the back of the clothespin. (Teacher step.)

Curriculum Connection
Language Arts

Discuss with students other legendary little characters (fairies, brownies, pixies, etc.). Create a large Venn diagram on a sheet of chart paper. Challenge your students to compare and contrast two different characters on the diagram.

Amy Barsanti • Roper, NC

St. Patty's Day Prints

Your lucky little leprechauns will love leaving their thumbprints on these adorable pins!

Materials (per child)

- frozen-juice can lid
- white construction paper circle (cut to fit lid)
- green stamp pad or tempera paint
- green magic marker
- pin back
- glue

Happy St. Patrick's Day!

Erin 2004

Directions

1. Glue the white circle to the juice can lid.
2. Make four green thumbprints on the white circle to create a shamrock shape.
3. Draw additional shamrock features with the green marker.
4. Write a St. Patrick's Day slogan on the white circle.
5. Glue the pin back to the back of the project.

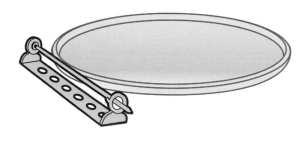

Curriculum Connection
Math

Give each pair of students a one-foot length of string with the ends tied together. In a designated grassy, outdoor area, direct each pair to lay the string in a circle atop the grass. Challenge each pair to count the number of clovers inside their string loop. Create a class graph with the findings.

Amy Barsanti • Roper, NC

Flying High

You will proudly fly this darling kite high in your classroom!

Materials (per child)

- copy of the kite pattern on page 135 enlarged on a 12" x 18" sheet of paper
- tagboard copy of the tail pattern on page 135
- 12" x 18" piece of craft foam
- four 3" squares of felt in different colors
- 24" length of yarn
- two 14" lengths of yarn
- craft jewels or sequins
- craft glue
- scissors
- marker

Directions

1. Cut out the enlarged kite pattern and trace it onto the foam. Cut out the kite shape.
2. Trace the tail pattern onto each of the four pieces of felt and cut them out.
3. Glue the tail pieces onto the 24-inch length of yarn, spacing evenly to create a kite tail. Let the glue dry.
4. Glue the remaining yarn pieces to the kite as shown.
5. Trim the yarn ends.
6. Glue craft jewels on the front of the kite.
7. Glue the kite tail to the back of the kite.

Curriculum Connection
Science

Benjamin Franklin once flew a kite in a storm to show the electrical nature of lightning. After sharing this fact, ask your youngsters to name other sources of electricity. Write their responses on chart paper. Invite each child to select a different source to research via the Internet. Have each child share his findings with the class.

Darcy Brown

Festival of Kites Mobile

Display this mobile where the kites can flutter in the breeze.

Materials (per child)

- plastic ring, cut from a container lid (approximately 6" in diameter)
- 4 lengths of string, varying from 12" to 36" in length
- four 12" lengths of yarn
- four 3" x 5" pieces of colored construction paper
- ribbon scraps
- glue
- scissors

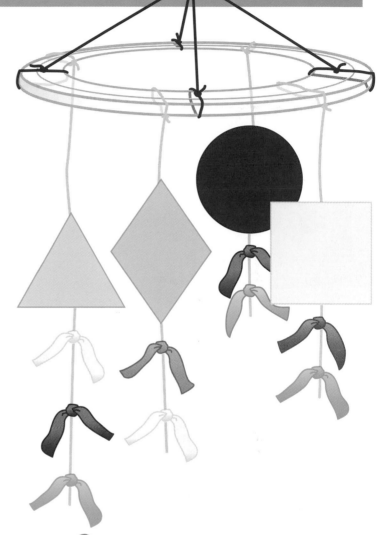

Directions

1. Cut a different basic shape from each of the construction paper pieces to create kites.
2. Glue each kite near the middle of a different length of string.
3. Tie ribbon scraps to the string below each kite shape to make a kite tail.
4. Tie the string ends to the plastic ring as shown.
5. Tie the four 12-inch lengths of yarn evenly across from one another on the ring.
6. Gather the four ends and tie them into a knot to form a hanger.

Curriculum Connection
Math

Review basic shapes with your students, such as those on the kite mobile. Then divide your class into small groups. Challenge each group to find objects in the classroom that have a matching shape. Have each group share its results with the class.

Linda Masternak Justice • Kansas City, MO

Mini Planter Pot

Teach your youngsters about recycling as they make this mini planter!

Materials (per child)

- clean bottle cap from liquid laundry soap
- mixture of white glue diluted with water in a bowl
- old magazines
- scraps of ribbon, lace, or rickrack
- glue
- paintbrush
- small gravel
- potting soil
- seeds
- scissors

Directions

1. Cut a flower picture from a magazine.
2. Paint a thin layer of glue mixture on the back of the picture.
3. With the bottle cap's opening facing up, gently press the picture onto the lower portion of the bottle cap. (If the bottle cap has grooves, press the picture into them.)
4. Repeat Steps 1–3, overlapping the pictures, until the entire bottle cap is covered.
5. Paint a thin layer of the diluted glue mixture over the pictures. Let it dry completely.
6. Glue ribbon bows, rickrack, or lace to the upper portion of the bottle cap.
7. Place a few gravel rocks into the bottom of the planter for drainage and then add soil and seeds.

Curriculum Connection
Science

After students have planted seeds in their mini planters, ask students to discuss other types of materials that can be recycled. Have each child pose the same question to family members. Complete a class graph that shows the types of items students recycle at home.

Linda Masternak Justice • Kansas City, MO

Garden Marker

This garden marker is just what you need for your springtime garden!

Materials (per child)

- wire coat hanger
- disposable clear plastic deli tray
- wooden bead
- 3" x 5" index card
- hole puncher
- wire cutters (for teacher use only)
- pliers (for teacher use only)
- permanent markers
- pencil
- scissors
- glue

Directions

1. In advance, use the wire cutters to cut the hanger as shown. Use the pliers to bend the end of the hanger, creating a hook. (Teacher step.)
2. Trace the index card onto a flat portion of the plastic tray. Cut out the plastic tag.
3. Punch a hole at the top of the tag.
4. Decorate the tag using the markers.
5. Slide the tag onto the hanger hook. Slide the wooden bead over the end of the hook and glue in place.

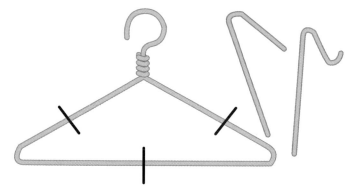

Linda Masternak Justice • Kansas City, MO

Curriculum Connection
Science
With prior permission from your school administrator, designate a plot of land as a garden for your youngsters. Have students help tend to the soil and plant a variety of flowers or vegetables. Invite each child to use his marker in the class garden.

You Are What You Eat

Help your youngsters make healthier food choices with this one-of-a-kind collage!

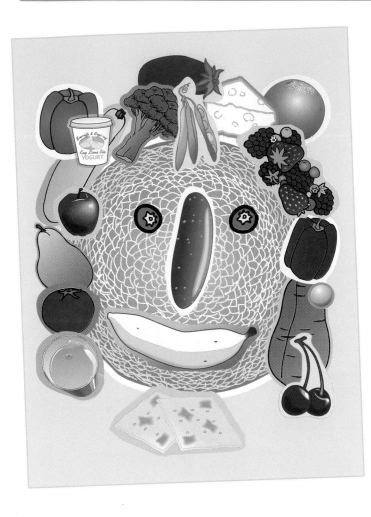

Materials (per child)

old magazines
12" x 18" sheet of construction
  paper
scissors
glue

Directions

1. Cut pictures of healthy food items from magazines.
2. Arrange the food pictures to make a face on the construction paper.
3. Glue the pictures in place on the paper.

Curriculum Connection
Health

After each child completes his picture, have students name the different food groups in his picture. Instruct each child to complete a graph that shows the total number in each food group. Display the graphs near the finished projects.

Linda Masternak Justice • Kansas City, MO

132

Hot-Air Balloon Bonanza

Transform your classroom into a brilliant hot-air balloon bonanza!

Materials (per child)

- copy of the balloon pattern on page 136
- two 9" x 12" sheets of colored paper
- colored paper scraps
- white paper
- cleaned half-pint milk carton with the top cut off
- paint mixture (1 tbsp. dish soap per 1 c. tempera paint)
- two 12" lengths of yarn
- paintbrush
- hole puncher
- stapler
- scissors
- pencil

Directions

1. Paint the milk carton with the paint mixture. Set it aside to dry.
2. Trace the balloon pattern onto the two pieces of paper. Cut out the shapes.
3. Use the colored paper scraps to decorate one side of each balloon shape.
4. Staple the balloons together decorated side out. (Leave an opening at the top.)
5. Gently stuff crumpled white paper into the balloon. Staple the hole closed.
6. Punch a hole through the bottom of the balloon.
7. Punch holes through two opposite sides of the milk carton.
8. Tie each yarn piece through a hole in the carton. Tie the other ends of the yarn through the hole in the balloon.

Curriculum Connection
Science

Show your students the following experiment to introduce how a hot-air balloon works. Place the open end of a balloon over a plastic liter bottle and set it in a bowl. Pour boiling water into the bowl (with students at a safe distance). Observe the results. Then carefully pour out the boiling water and replace it with ice cubes. Have students note the change. Now they'll know why it's called a hot-air balloon!

Mary Richard • St. Augustine, FL

Shamrock Man Patterns
Use with "Shamrock Man" on page 125.

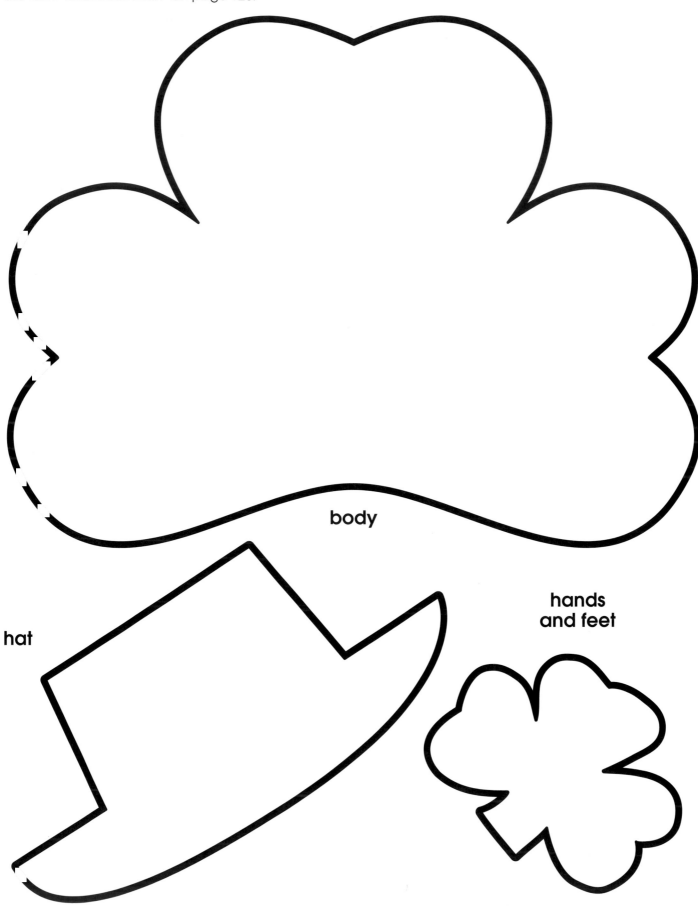

body

hat

hands
and feet

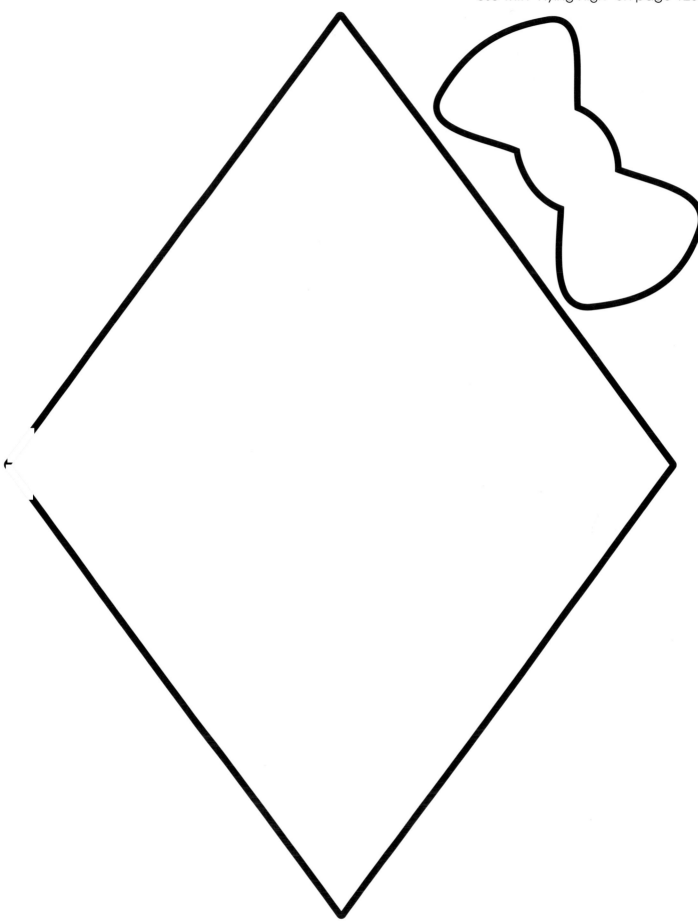

Balloon Pattern
Use with "Hot-Air Balloon Bonanza" on page 133.

APRIL

Rainy-Day Picture

That's not rain…it's salt!

Materials (per child)

9" x 12" sheet of white
   construction paper
pencil
watercolor paints
paintbrush
salt

Directions

1. Lightly pencil an outdoor scene on the paper.
2. Paint the design with the watercolor paints.
3. While the paint is still wet, sprinkle salt atop the picture. Let the paint dry.
4. Gently brush off the salt.

Curriculum Connection
Communication Skills

Read aloud *The Cat in the Hat* by Dr. Seuss. After sharing this rainy-day tale, ask each child to tell what she would do if this famous cat made an appearance at her house on a rainy day.

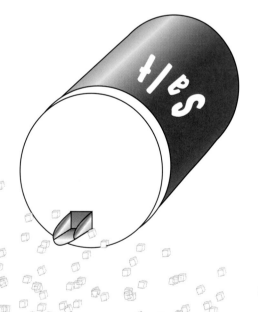

Cindy Barber • Fredonia, WI

Rain Globe

Bring the rain into your classroom with a simple shake of this rain globe!

Materials (per child)

- clear plastic jar with lid
- ¾ c. water, lightly tinted with blue food coloring
- spoonful of blue glitter
- small plastic duck (to fit inside jar)
- hot glue gun (for teacher use only)

Directions

1. Hot-glue the small duck to the inside of the jar lid (teacher step).
2. Pour the spoonful of glitter into the jar.
3. Fill the jar with the tinted water.
4. Hot-glue the lid to the jar (teacher step).
5. Turn jar to stir up the rain.

Curriculum Connection
Writing

Invite each child to write a rainy-day acrostic poem. Direct each child to write "RAIN" vertically down a sheet of white construction paper. Have him write one descriptive word or phrase for each letter in the word. Display the poems on a bulletin board titled "Rainy-Day Acrostics."

Heather E. Graley • Columbus, OH

Puffy Rainbow

Brighten your classroom with this puffy rainbow!

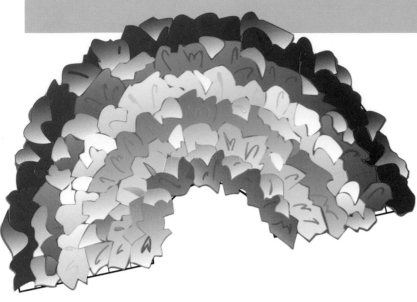

Materials (per child)

- 9" x 12" piece of clear Con-Tact covering
- 12 four-inch squares each of red, orange, yellow, green, blue, and purple tissue paper
- permanent marker
- scissors

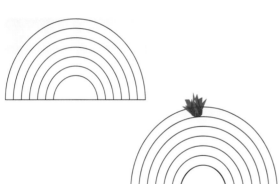

Directions

1. With the marker, draw a rainbow with six layers on the clear side of the Con-Tact covering.
2. Cut out the shape.
3. Carefully peel off the protective backing.
4. Place the rainbow on a flat surface, sticky side up.
5. Wrap a square of tissue paper around the end of your finger and press the tissue onto the appropriate section of the rainbow.
6. Repeat Step 5 until the rainbow is covered with paper.
7. Gently fluff the tissue.

Curriculum Connection
Writing

Stimulate your youngsters' minds with the following writing prompt: One day, after a rain shower, you see an upside-down rainbow. Challenge each child to write about what happens the day a flip-flopped rainbow appears in the sky.

Cindy Barber • Fredonia, WI

Shiny Rainbows

These unique rainbows are sure to reflect your students' individuality!

Materials (per child)

- Shiny paint in red, orange, yellow, green, blue, and purple; made by mixing the following ingredients:
  - 2 tbsp. corn syrup
  - 1½ tsp. water
  - ¼ tsp. baking soda
  - ¼ tsp. cornstarch
  - 3 or more drops food coloring
- 8" x 8" tagboard square
- paintbrushes
- scissors
- hole puncher
- yarn

Directions

1. Have each child paint the square with stripes of shiny paint in the order of a rainbow.
2. Allow the paint to dry completely (at least four hours).
3. Cut a large shape—such as a star, cloud, or heart—from the painted square. (Be sure to include all of the colors.)
4. Punch a hole at the top of the cutout.
5. Tie a length of yarn through the hole.

Curriculum Connection
Science

Have students explore rainbows with bubbles! On a sunny day, take your youngsters outside. Have pairs of students blow bubbles into the sunlight. Explain to your students that the rainbows they see are created by the reflection of the sun off the bubbles.

Susie Kapaun • Orchard Park, NY

"Symme-tree"

Create a forest in your classroom with a class collection of these "symme-trees"!

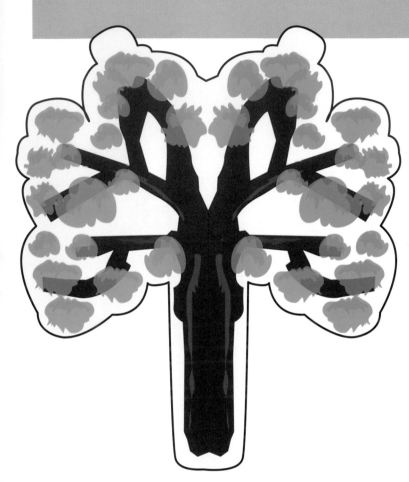

Materials (per child)

- 9" x 12" sheet of white construction paper
- brown and green tempera paint
- paintbrushes
- scissors

Directions

1. Fold the construction paper in half lengthwise. Unfold the paper.
2. Paint one-half of a tree trunk and branches near the crease on one side of the paper.
3. Fold the paper in half and press the sides together. Unfold the paper.
4. Let the paint dry completely.
5. Paint dots of green leaves on one half of the tree.
6. Fold the paper in half and press the sides together. Unfold the paper.
7. When the paint has dried, trim around the tree.

Curriculum Connection
Science
Ask students to name items in nature that are symmetrical. Have students repeat the art activity to create butterflies, flowers, leaves, or other symmetrical natural shapes.

Cynthia Holcomb • Mertzon, TX

Bubble-Wrap Egg

Add sparkle to any display with this uniquely textured egg. Wow!

Materials (per child)

- 6" square of bubble wrap
- tagboard copy of the egg pattern on page 156
- white construction paper
- red, yellow, and blue food coloring
- 3 small containers of water
- 3 eyedroppers
- assorted glitter colors
- toothpick
- paintbrush
- scissors
- scallop-edged scissors
- glue
- pencil

Directions

1. Trace the egg pattern on the bubble wrap. Cut out the shape.
2. Tint each of the three containers of water with a different food coloring.
3. Paint the bubbled side of the egg cutout with glue.
4. Place a few drops of each water color onto the egg.
5. Spread and blend the colors together with the toothpick.
6. While the glue is still wet, sprinkle the glitter atop the egg. Let the glue dry completely.
7. Glue the white construction paper to the undecorated side of the egg.
8. Trim the paper around the egg with the scallop-edged scissors.

Mackie Rhodes • Greensboro, NC

Curriculum Connection
Writing

Ask each youngster to imagine his egg has magical powers. Invite him to write a story about his magical egg. Display the writings near the eggs for a sparkly Easter display.

A-tisket, A-tasket

A-tisket, a-tasket…it's so much fun to make this basket!

Materials (per child)

- manila folder
- craft knife (teacher use only)
- large piece of sturdy cardboard
- assorted 12" strips of yarn, string, cording, ribbon, fabric, and/or paper
- shredded colored paper
- glue
- scissors

Directions

1. Cut a trapezoid shape from the manila folder to form a basket as shown. Then cut a strip from the remaining folder scraps for a handle. Lay the unfolded basket atop the cardboard and use the craft knife to cut slits as shown. (teacher step only)
2. Weave the strips of various materials over and under the slits in the basket. Trim away excess weaving material.
3. Refold the basket and glue the two sides together. Let the glue dry.
4. Glue the handle to each side of the basket.
5. Fill the basket with shredded paper.

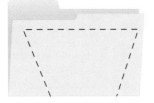

Curriculum Connection
Language Arts

After the project, teach your youngsters the words to the famous nursery rhyme "A-tisket, A-tasket." Invite students to parade around the room holding their baskets as they recite the rhyme.

Linda Masternak Justice • Kansas City, MO

144

Great Golden Egg

Your youngsters will love to re-create this classic golden egg!

Materials (per child)

- foam egg
- several assorted gold foil candy wrappers
- craft sequins, rhinestones, or jewels
- paintbrush
- craft glue

Directions

1. Paint a thin layer of glue atop the egg.
2. Gently overlap the candy wrappers atop the glue.
3. Glue sequins or other craft jewels to the egg.

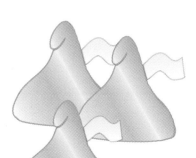

Curriculum Connection
Reading

Read aloud your favorite version of *The Goose That Laid the Golden Egg*. Encourage each student to retell the story at home using her golden egg creation as a prop.

Linda Masternak Justice • Kansas City, MO

Marbled Egg

Try this unique idea for an "egg-citing" approach to Easter decorations!

Materials (per child)

- copy of the egg pattern on page 156 enlarged to fit a 9" x 12" sheet of paper
- 9" x 12" sheet of white construction paper
- colored chalk
- straw or toothpick
- cookie sheet
- water
- grater
- aerosol hairspray (for teacher use only)
- scissors
- pencil

Directions

1. Trace the egg pattern on the white construction paper and cut it out.
2. Pour water into the cookie sheet so it just covers the bottom.
3. Using the smallest holes in the grater, grate different colors of chalk over the water.
4. Use the straw or toothpick to gently swirl the chalk shavings in the water.
5. Carefully place the egg cutout on top of the water.
6. Gently peel the egg off the water. Let it dry completely.
7. Spray the egg with the hairspray in a ventilated area. (teacher step only)

Curriculum Connection
Communication Skills

Read aloud Robert D. San Souci's book The Talking Eggs. Invite each child to imagine what it might be like to have a talking egg. Have her tell a partner what her egg would say.

Cindy Barber • Fredonia, WI

Bonny Bonnet

This bonny Easter bonnet will add plenty of charm to your classroom!

Materials (per child)

- foam cup
- scraps of lace
- ribbon
- miniature silk flowers
- permanent markers
- craft glue
- cookie sheet
- oven (for teacher use only)

Directions

1. Have your teacher bake and shape the cup using the baking directions below.
2. When the cup has cooled, glue ribbon, lace, and/or flowers around the hat.
3. Use the markers to decorate the outside of the cup if desired.

Baking Directions (only an adult should perform the following):

1. Preheat the cookie sheet and the oven to 250 degrees.
2. Place up to four inverted cups at one time in a circle near the middle of the baking sheet.
3. Heat the cups for no more than one to two minutes. (Watch as they bake if possible.)
4. Remove the cups from the oven and immediately shape them gently into hats with your fingers.

Curriculum Connection
Language Arts
Chapeau means "hat" in French. Challenge students to find the French words for other common objects. Display the findings on a classroom chart.

VaReane Gray Heese • Omaha, NE

Bunny Stick Puppet

Your students will love using this stick puppet to act out favorite bunny songs!

Materials (per child)

- wide craft stick
- white tempera paint
- paintbrush
- fingertip from a discarded knit glove
- 2" square of white construction paper
- markers
- scissors
- craft glue
- ribbon

Directions

1. Paint both sides of the craft stick white. Set aside to dry.
2. Roll up the cut edge of the glove tip to form a hat.
3. Slide the hat atop one end of the craft stick and glue it in place.
4. Cut two small bunny ears from the white paper and glue them to the hat.
5. Use the markers to decorate the ears and to add facial details.
6. Wrap the ribbon around the bunny and tie it into a bow. Secure the bow to the bunny with a dot of glue.

Curriculum Connection
Math

Challenge pairs of students to write a bunny-related word problem for one another. Have students swap problems. Invite each child to use her puppet to relay her answer to her partner.

Amy Barsanti • Roper, NC

Bunny Bag

Fill this adorable bag with Easter grass and goodies for a treat that "every-bunny" is sure to love!

Materials (per child)

- paper lunch sack
- 3 large buttons (1 pink and 2 blue)
- six 3" pieces of raffia
- pink construction paper scraps
- scissors
- glue
- marker

Directions

1. Lay the paper sack flat.
2. Cut out the top section of the sack as shown to form the ears.
3. Cut the pink construction paper to fit inside the ears.
4. Glue the cutouts to the middle of the ears.
5. Glue the buttons to the sack to make eyes and a nose.
6. Glue the raffia around the nose for whiskers.
7. Use the marker to draw additional facial features on the bag.

Curriculum Connection
Science

Place an object in a bunny bag. Have students, in turn, reach into the bag without looking, touch the object, and guess the object's identity. Repeat using a variety of objects to increase sensory awareness.

VaReane Gray Heese • Omaha, NE

Curious Cottontail

Where is that curious bunny going? This little cutie lends itself to a creative-writing activity.

Materials (per child)

- white 5 oz. paper cup
- 2½" foam ball
- cotton ball
- pink and white craft foam
- permanent markers
- shredded green paper or Easter grass
- scissors
- pencil
- craft glue

Directions

1. Draw spring designs on the white cup with the markers.
2. Fill the cup with the shredded paper or Easter grass so that some is hanging over the edge.
3. Line the cup rim with glue and press the foam ball into the cup. Let the glue dry.
4. Glue the cotton ball to the foam ball for a tail.
5. With the pencil, draw bunny paws (about one inch in diameter) on the white foam. Cut the pieces out.
6. Draw bunny paw pads on the pink foam. Cut the pieces out.
7. Glue the pink pieces to the bunny feet.
8. Glue the bunny feet below the tail.

Curriculum Connection
Creative Writing

Invite your youngsters to find out what happened to another curious cottontail by sharing the story *The Tale of Peter Rabbit* by Beatrix Potter. After hearing the tale, ask each child to make a list of things that got Peter into trouble. Then have each child make a list of things children are curious about.

Susie Kapaun • Orchard Park, NY

Spring Chick

This little chick is ready to peep its way into your heart!

Materials (per child)

- foam egg
- 4 yellow craft feathers
- two 2 mm black pom-poms
- 12" orange pipe cleaner
- 8 or 10 cotton balls (yellow if available)
- yellow tempera paint
- paintbrush
- ruler
- scissors
- glue

Directions

1. Paint the egg yellow. Let the paint dry.
2. Measure and cut a one-inch piece of pipe cleaner. Fold the piece in half and insert the resulting beak into one side of the egg.
3. Cut the remaining piece of pipe cleaner in half. Twist each piece into a foot as shown.
4. Insert both feet into the wide bottom of the egg.
5. Glue the cotton balls to the chick, leaving the face uncovered.
6. Glue two feathers to the chick for wings. Glue the remaining feathers to the back for a tail.
7. Glue the black pom-poms to the face for eyes.

Curriculum Connection
Science

Ask your students which they think came first—the chicken or the egg. Complete a class graph that shows the results of the survey. Challenge students to write math sentences to describe the finished graph.

Linda Masternak Justice • Kansas City, MO

Bye-Bye Birdie

It's time for this little birdie to spread its wings!

Materials (per child)

- ¼ c. rice
- 2 tbsp. glue
- 2 tbsp. brown tempera paint
- small yogurt container
- plastic spoon
- plastic knife
- raffia
- pom-pom
- 2 small wiggle eyes
- three ½" pieces of orange pipe cleaner
- craft feather
- scissors
- glue

Directions

1. Mix the glue and the paint together.
2. Mix the rice and the glue mixture in the yogurt container. Press the mixture into the bottom of the cup with the spoon, creating a nestlike shape. Let it dry.
3. Use the plastic knife to loosen the nest from the inside of the cup and gently pop it out.
4. Cut the raffia into short pieces. Glue the pieces inside the nest.
5. Glue the pipe cleaner pieces (beak and legs) and the wiggle eyes to the pom-pom (bird).
6. Cut a craft feather to make two wings and a tail. Glue each one onto the bird body.
7. When the glue has dried, glue the bird onto the edge of the nest facing outward.

Mackie Rhodes • Greensboro, NC

Curriculum Connection Communication Skills

Ask each youngster to tell a partner about the day his little bird learned to fly. For an added challenge, have each youngster tell his story from the bird's point of view.

Birdhouse Bag

This whimsical birdhouse may not attract real birds, but it's sure to be a hit!

Materials (per child)

- paper lunch sack
- 1' length of twine
- shredded paper
- raffia
- small twig
- 5" x 8" piece of construction paper
- markers
- craft glue
- scissors
- hole puncher
- stapler
- sharpened pencil

Directions

1. Cut the lunch sack in half.
2. Flatten the top half, and glue the construction paper between the layers for durability.
3. Fold this glued piece vertically in half to form the roof.
4. Draw roof details on the bag.
5. Open the bottom portion of the bag and stuff it lightly with shredded paper.
6. Pinch the open edges of the filled bag together and staple shut.
7. Place the roof atop the stapled bag.
8. Punch a hole through the center of all the layers.
9. Thread the twine through the punched hole and tie it to make a hanger.
10. Use a pencil to poke a small hole in the side of the stuffed bag for a birdhouse door.
11. Glue the raffia and the twig in the hole.

VaReane Gray Heese • Omaha, NE

Curriculum Connection
Science

Look for an abandoned bird nest to observe. Record all the items your class sees in the nest. Challenge students to determine how many of these items birds could use again next spring.

Baseball Magnet

Here's a cool sports magnet for attaching your favorite team photo to the refrigerator!

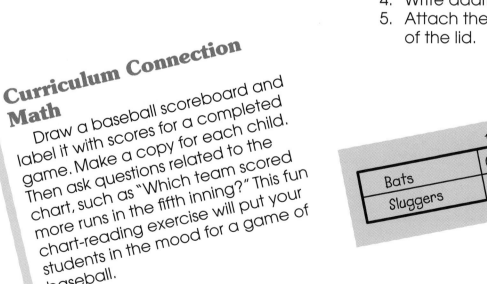

I ♥ Baseball

Materials (per child)

- clean frozen juice can lid
- white tempera paint
- red tempera paint
- paintbrushes
- red fine-point permanent marker
- one 2" piece of magnetic tape
- small wooden heart
- craft glue

Directions

1. Paint the juice can lid white. Let the paint dry.
2. Draw baseball stitching lines on the lid with the marker.
3. Paint the heart red and glue it onto the lid.
4. Write additional lettering on the lid.
5. Attach the magnetic strip to the back of the lid.

Curriculum Connection
Math

Draw a baseball scoreboard and label it with scores for a completed game. Make a copy for each child. Then ask questions related to the chart, such as "Which team scored more runs in the fifth inning?" This fun chart-reading exercise will put your students in the mood for a game of baseball.

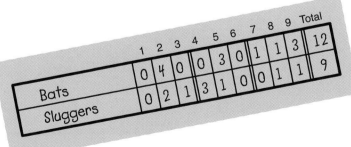

	1	2	3	4	5	6	7	8	9	Total
Bats	0	4	0	0	3	0	1	1	3	12
Sluggers	0	2	1	3	1	0	0	1	1	9

Colleen Dabney • Williamsburg, VA

Baseball Treat

Here's a unique edible treat to culminate your baseball unit!

Materials (per child)

- round sugar cookie
- white frosting
- red gel icing (in a tube)
- red string licorice
- plastic knife
- scissors

Directions

1. Use the knife to spread the frosting on the surface of the cookie.
2. Cut two lengths of licorice (slightly longer than the diameter of the cookie).
3. Press each piece of licorice into the frosting as shown.
4. Draw laces with the red tube icing.

Curriculum Connection
Reading
Read aloud *Casey at the Bat* by Ernest Lawrence Thayer. As you are sharing the story, invite your youngsters to munch on their mouthwatering baseball treats.

Susie Kapaun • Orchard Park, NY

Egg Pattern

Use with "Bubble-Wrap Egg" on page 143 and "Marbled Egg" on page 146.

MAY

Terrific Tulip

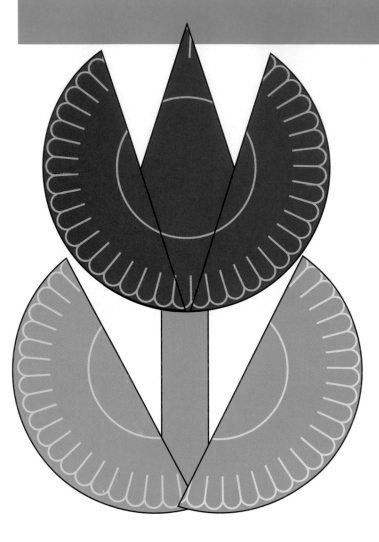

Welcome spring with a burst of these colorful blooms!

Materials (per child)

- two 6" paper plates
- tempera paints
- paintbrush
- pencil
- scissors
- glue

Directions

1. Paint one paper plate in a desired color. Let the paint dry.
2. Use a pencil to draw lines on the painted plate as shown.
3. Cut the plate apart along the lines.
4. Arrange the pieces together to form a tulip blossom. Glue the pieces together and set it aside.
5. Paint the other paper plate green. Let the paint dry.
6. Cut a one-inch strip from the middle of the green plate as shown.
7. Glue the strip (stem) to the back of the flower.
8. Glue the remaining green pieces (leaves) to the bottom of the stem.

Curriculum Connection
Math

Have students use their flowers in a graphing activity. Staple the flowers to a bulletin board in rows by color. After enlisting students' help in labeling the resulting graph, challenge each youngster to write a question that can be answered with the information.

Step 2

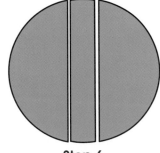

Step 6

Cynthia Holcomb • Mertzon, TX

Royal Rose Bouquet

These royal roses are fit for a queen…or king!

Materials (per child)

- 3 sterilized foam egg carton sections
- three 12" green pipe cleaners
- 6" length of red ribbon
- red tempera paint with dish soap added
- paintbrush
- sharpened pencil

Directions

1. Paint the inside and outside of each egg carton section red. Let the paint dry.
2. With the pencil, poke a hole through the bottom of each section.
3. Insert approximately two inches of a different pipe cleaner (stem) through the bottom of each egg carton section (flower).
4. Twist the stem inside each flower so it will not pull out.
5. Gather the stems together and tie a ribbon bow to make a bouquet.

Curriculum Connection
Creative Writing

Ask each child to imagine what life might be like as a king or queen. Challenge each student to write a descriptive paragraph that tells about this royal life. Invite each youngster to share his paragraph with his classmates.

Laura L. Wagner • Austin, TX

Dilly Daffodil

This dilly daffodil is sure to have your classroom a-bloomin'!

Materials (per child)

- 2 white pleated paper condiment cups
- soda straw
- six 1" lengths of yellow yarn
- green construction paper scraps
- sharpened pencil
- yellow marker or crayon
- glue
- scissors

Directions

1. Color the inside and outside of each condiment cup yellow.
2. Gently pull apart the pleats of one cup and slightly flatten.
3. Glue the pleated cup to the middle of the flattened cup.
4. Use the pencil to poke a hole in the center of the glued cups.
5. Gather the yarn lengths together. Glue the ends of the lengths inside one end of the straw. Let the glue dry completely.
6. Push the other end of the straw through the hole in the cups.
7. Cut leaves from the green construction paper scraps and glue them to the straw.

Curriculum Connection
Science

Daffodils are plants that grow in the springtime. Ask your youngsters to name other flowers that bloom in the spring. List their responses on a sheet of chart paper. Challenge each child to research a different flower from the list.

Linda Masternak Justice • Kansas City, MO

Peekaboo Garden

Give your students a peek at what goes on *under* a garden with this three-dimensional diagram!

Materials (per child)

- 9" paper plate
- three ½ cm black pom-poms
- five ½ cm pink pom-poms
- colored construction paper scraps
- white yarn scraps
- scissors
- crayons or markers
- glue

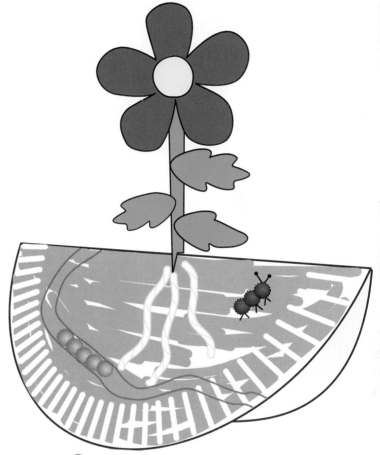

Directions

1. Color the paper plate brown.
2. Fold the plate in half, colored side out.
3. Cut a one-inch slit into the top of the folded edge.
4. Cut a flower and stem from the construction paper scraps and glue the pieces together.
5. When the glue has dried, insert the flower into the slit.
6. Cut lengths of yarn (roots) and glue them beneath the flower on each side of the plate.
7. Glue the pink pom-poms (worm) and the black pom-poms (ant) to the plate.
8. Draw additional underground features, such as insects, rocks, and tunnels.

Curriculum Connection
Science

Divide students into small groups. Instruct each group to use materials such as encyclopedias and the Internet to research a different topic, like how worms help gardens. Challenge each group to creatively present its findings to the class.

Cynthia Holcomb • Mertzon, TX

Stick Fish

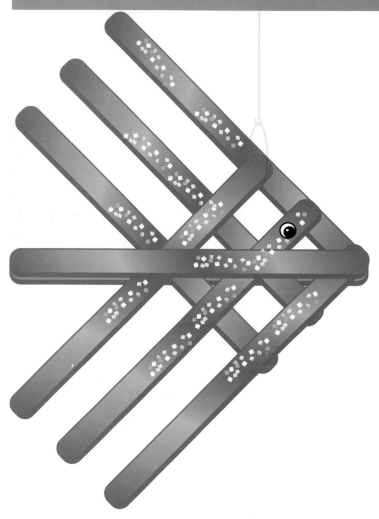

Reel in your students—hook, line, and sinker—with this fantastic fish project!

Materials (per child)

- 8 craft sticks
- 2 wiggle eyes
- tempera paint
- 6" piece of monofilament line
- glitter
- glue
- paintbrush

Directions

1. Arrange a row of three craft sticks as shown.
2. Arrange and glue another row of three craft sticks perpendicular to the first row as shown. Let the glue dry.
3. Glue a single craft stick atop the others as shown. Let the glue dry.
4. Turn the fish over and glue the remaining craft stick on the opposite side of the fish.
5. Paint one side of the fish.
6. While the paint is still wet, sprinkle a layer of glitter atop it.
7. Repeat Steps 5 and 6 on the unpainted side to complete the fish.
8. Glue a wiggle eye to each side of the fish.
9. Thread the monofilament line through the top of the fish and tie the ends together.

Curriculum Connection
Science

Have student volunteers research and write fish facts on index cards. Display the index cards and the finished projects on a bulletin board titled "Fishy Facts."

Cynthia Holcomb • Mertzon, TX

Friendly Fish

Let's go fishing for a friendly fish string puppet!

Materials (per child)

- two 9" paper plates
- 2 wiggle eyes
- 3 coffee filters
- watercolor paints
- small bowl of water
- paintbrush
- craft stick
- hole puncher
- 24" length of yarn
- scissors
- glue

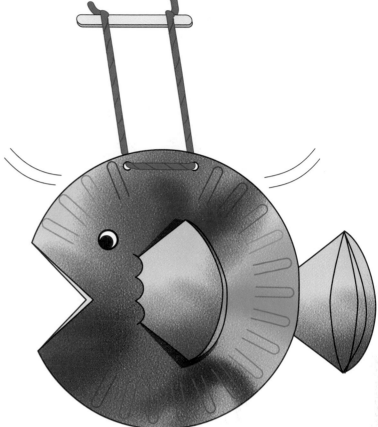

Directions

1. Hold the plates together, bottom sides out, and cut a triangular notch through both plates to form a mouth.
2. Cut a scalloped slit (gill) behind the mouth on each plate.
3. Paint the bottom side of each plate and each coffee filter with the watercolor paints. Let the paint dry.
4. Fold a filter into fourths, then insert the pointed end into the gill on one plate. Fold the point of the filter back and glue it to the plate.
5. Repeat Step 4 using a second filter and the other plate.
6. Glue one wiggle eye to each plate.
7. Fold the last filter (tail) and glue the point to the inside edge of one plate, opposite the mouth.
8. Glue the two plates along the edges.
9. Punch two holes at the top of the fish.
10. Thread the yarn through the holes and tie the ends to the craft stick.

Julie A. Koczur

Curriculum Connection
Writing

Challenge small groups of students to write a short play in which the main characters are fish. Invite each group to perform its play for the class using the friendly fish puppets.

Window Aquarium

Create an ocean in your classroom with this window aquarium!

Materials (per child)

9" x 12" sheet of colored
   construction paper
laminating machine (for teacher
   use only) or clear Con-Tact
   paper
construction paper scraps
permanent markers
scissors
glue

Directions

1. Fold the construction paper in half.
2. Cut out the inside portion of the paper, leaving approximately a one-inch border.
3. Unfold the paper and laminate it. (Teacher step only.)
4. Trim the edges of the laminating film.
5. Cut aquarium creatures and other details, such as rocks and plants, from the construction paper scraps.
6. Glue the pictures atop the laminating film inside the aquarium border.
7. Add additional aquarium details using permanent markers.
8. Display the aquarium in your classroom window.

Curriculum Connection
Science and Character Education

Instill a little responsibility in your students by enlisting their help with maintaining a classroom aquarium. Decide on a place and size for your aquarium. With the youngsters' help, fill the aquarium with rocks, plants, fish, and water. Set up a schedule for students to assist in feeding the fish and cleaning the aquarium.

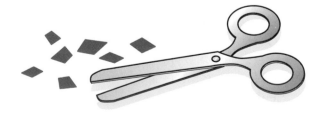

Michelle McCormick • Holdrege, NE

Inky

This whimsical windsock will ink its way into your heart!

Materials (per child)

- 12" x 18" sheet of purple construction paper
- four 2½' lengths of black crepe paper
- three 12" lengths of yarn
- construction paper scraps
- hole puncher
- scissors
- glue
- stapler

Directions

1. Cut a 9" x 18" piece from the purple construction paper. Set the piece aside.
2. Cut eight wavy legs from the remaining piece of construction paper.
3. Evenly space the legs and glue them onto the long side of the 9" x 18" piece of paper.
4. Cut two eyes from the construction paper scraps and glue them to the middle of the paper.
5. Roll the paper into a cylinder. Secure the short ends of the paper with glue.
6. Staple the four lengths of crepe paper to the bottom back of the octopus.
7. Punch three evenly spaced holes near the top of the octopus.
8. Tie one end of each yarn length to a different hole.
9. Gather the remaining yarn ends together and tie them into a knot.

Valerie Wood Smith • Morgantown, PA

Curriculum Connection
Literature

Read aloud *An Octopus Is Amazing* by Patricia Lauber. After sharing the book, invite each student to name one interesting fact she learned about the octopus. Write the responses on a sheet of chart paper. Display the chart and the book in your language arts center for further reading.

June Bug

Students will go buggy over this painting project!

Materials (per child)

- 6" x 9" sheet of white paper
- 7" x 10" sheet of colorful construction paper
- tempera paints
- paintbrushes
- black marker
- glue stick

Directions

1. Fold the white paper in half.
2. Unfold the paper.
3. Dip a paintbrush into a desired paint color. Randomly dab the paint onto one side of the creased paper.
4. Repeat Step 3 with other colors of paint.
5. Fold the paper in half again, gently pressing the sides together.
6. Unfold the paper. Let the paint dry completely.
7. Draw bug features on the paint splotch with the marker.
8. Glue the bug painting to the sheet of construction paper.

Curriculum Connection
Math
Discuss symmetry with your students using their bug paintings as examples.

Amy Barsanti • Roper, NC

Buggy Fan

What better way to beat the heat than with this adorable buggy fan!

Materials (per child)

- colorful construction paper
    copy of the bug and wing
    patterns on page 174
- tracing paper
- large craft stick
- black marker
- pencil
- scissors
- glue

Directions

1. Cut out the bug body.
2. Use the marker to add details to the bug body.
3. Lay the tracing paper atop the wing patterns. Trace the outline of the patterns with the pencil.
4. Cut the wings out of the tracing paper.
5. Glue the tracing paper wings to the bug.
6. Glue the craft stick at the head of the bug, as shown, to make a fan.

Curriculum Connection Science

Encourage your students to experiment with the effects of air flow. Ask each child to test and observe whether faster or slower fanning results in cooler or more air being circulated.

VaReane Gray Heese • Omaha, NE

Tongue-Flicking Frog

Students will be hoppin' to try on this frog mask!

Materials (per child)

- one 9" paper plate
- tongue depressor
- 2 white construction paper copies of the eye patterns on page 175
- green tempera paint
- green crayon   sharpened pencil
- paintbrush   permanent
- scissors   marker
- glue   party blower

Directions

1. Paint the bottom of the paper plate green.
2. Color the half-circle eye patterns green; then cut out all of the eye patterns.
3. Glue the eye pieces to the plate as shown.
4. Cut through the eyes and the plate where indicated.
5. Use the pencil to poke a hole approximately three inches from the bottom of the plate.
6. Draw a smile on the plate incorporating the pencil hole.
7. Enlarge the hole in the mouth, then insert and glue the blower into position.
8. Glue the tongue depressor to the back of the frog.
9. Blow into the blower to flick the frog's tongue.

Curriculum Connection
Communication Skills

Encourage groups of students to write frog songs. Then have them perform the songs while wearing their masks.

Mackie Rhodes • Greensboro, NC

Stand-Up Frog

This happy fellow will make a nice addition to your environmental display!

Materials (per child)

- green construction paper copy of the frog pattern on page 175
- white construction paper copy of the frog pattern on page 175
- 4" length of red curling ribbon
- crayons   sharpened pencil
- glue stick   scissors
- tape

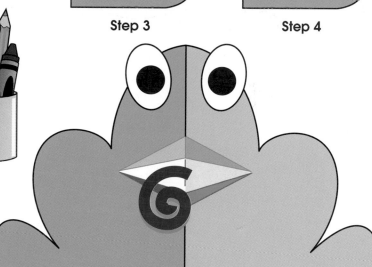

Step 3   Step 4

Directions

1. Cut out the frog patterns.
2. Fold the green frog pattern along the dotted line (dotted line out).
3. Cut a 1" horizontal slit into the fold of the paper at the dot.
4. Fold back two triangles to the right and left of the slit. Press the crease lines heavily.
5. Unfold the triangles back to their original positions. Push the folded triangles to the inside of the folded pattern.
6. Use the pencil to poke a small hole through the dot on the white frog pattern.
7. Unfold the green frog pattern.
8. Glue the green frog atop the white frog, along the edges.
9. Cut two frog eyes from the scraps of white paper and glue them to the frog.
10. Insert the length of curling ribbon (tongue) through the hole in the mouth.
11. Tape the tongue to the back of the frog.
12. Decorate the frog as desired.
13. Fold the frog vertically to make the mouth open.

Cynthia G. Holzschuher • Lebanon, OH

Curriculum Connection Communication Skills

As a class, sing aloud your favorite version of a frog ditty, such as "Five Green and Speckled Frogs." Challenge students to make up a fingerplay to go with the words of the song. After singing and performing the fingerplay, invite each child to illustrate a picture that depicts a verse of the song.

Bandana Brands

Your youngsters will enjoy decorating their very own bandanas!

Materials (per child)

- 24" square of cloth (at least 60 percent synthetic)
- 24" square of paper
- pinking shears (for teacher use only)
- iron (for teacher use only)
- fabric crayons
- pencil
- black marker

Directions

1. Cut along each edge of the fabric square with the pinking shears. (Teacher step only.)
2. With the pencil, design brand symbols on the square of paper.
3. Trace over the design with the marker.
4. Flip the paper over. Trace over the marker lines with the fabric crayons.
5. Place the paper, crayon side down, atop the fabric square.
6. Iron the design onto the fabric according to the directions on the fabric crayon box. (Teacher step only.)

Curriculum Connection
Literature

Before students design their bandanas, share one of these stories with them. The information is sure to inspire the cowpoke inside each of them to design a fantastic bandana!

- *A Brand Is Forever* by Ann Herbert Scott
- *Why Cowboys Need a Brand* by Laurie Lazzaro Knowlton

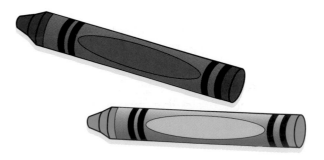

Linda Masternak Justice • Kansas City, MO

170

Ten-Gallon Hat

Round up your little buckaroos with these ten-gallon hats!

Materials (per child)

- 6½" tall clay or plastic pot, sand pail, or bucket
- 24" square of craft paper
- water-thinned glue
- undiluted glue
- kite string
- sheet of waxed paper
- large paintbrush   24" ribbon
- scissors   craft feather

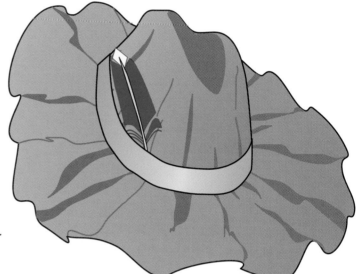

Directions

1. Set the pot upright in the middle of the paper square.
2. Wrap the paper snugly around the pot, tucking the edges inside. (This will create the top of the hat.)
3. Turn the pot over onto the waxed paper. Tie a length of string around the bottom of the pot. (Teacher note: For a child with a larger head, tie the string loosely around the pot.)
4. Coat the paper with the water-thinned glue. Let the glue dry.
5. Pull out the paper tucked in the pot. Spread the paper out to make a hat brim.
6. Paint the entire hat with the undiluted glue. Let the glue dry.
7. Lift the hat off the pot.
8. Trim the edges of the brim to resemble a cowboy hat. Then gently dent the top of the hat.
9. Glue the ribbon around the base of the hat, covering the string.
10. Tuck the feather between the hat and the band and glue it in place.

Mackie Rhodes • Greensboro, NC

Curriculum Connection Communication Skills

Set the stage for a cowpoke campfire. Arrange the students' chairs in a circle around a pretend fire made from cardboard tube logs and tissue paper flames. Invite the students to don their hats as they join you around the campfire. Dim the lights; then have everyone join in as you all sing your favorite campfire songs.

Fiesta Dolls

This fiesta doll will be the talk of your Cinco de Mayo festivities!

Materials (per child)

- rounded wooden clothespin
- yarn, string, or embroidery thread
- fabric scraps or ribbon (for girl doll)
- 4" length of pipe cleaner
- markers
- scissors
- glue

Directions

1. Draw facial features on the clothespin head.
2. Glue the length of pipe cleaner (arms) to the back of the clothespin.
3. Secure the arms in place by wrapping the yarn crisscross around the clothespin as shown.
4. Use the following steps to make a boy or girl doll.

Boy:
— Wrap the yarn around the body and down each leg separately.
— Draw hair and shoes on the doll with the markers.

Girl:
— Wrap the yarn around the body and down the legs together.
— Cut a small triangle (kerchief) from the fabric scraps.
— Glue the kerchief to the head.
— Cut a 1" x 2" strip (skirt) from the fabric scraps.
— Glue the skirt around the waist.

Linda Masternak Justice • Kansas City, MO

Curriculum Connection
Social Studies

Cinco de Mayo is a celebration of a historic victory among people of Mexican heritage. Share literature related to Cinco de Mayo; then invite parents and students of Mexican descent to share their Cinco de Mayo experiences and traditions with your class.

Fiesta Sun

This sun will surely shine on your fiesta!

Materials (per child)

- 3 colorful paper copies (orange, red, and yellow) of the sun patterns on page 176
- 6" paper plate
- scraps of yellow construction paper
- markers
- glue
- scissors

Directions

1. Tear the construction paper scraps into irregular pieces.
2. Glue the pieces, overlapping them, on the front of the paper plate.
3. Cut out the sun pattern strips.
4. Fold the paper strips as shown.
5. Glue an outer row of folded strips around the perimeter of the plate.
6. Glue a second row inside and overlapping the first row.
7. Let the glue dry completely.
8. Draw a face on the sun with the markers.

Curriculum Connection
Social Studies

Challenge your students to duplicate Mexican tin work. Provide each child with an aluminum pie pan. Have him draw a design on a paper circle the same size as the bottom of the pan. Then direct him to duplicate his design on the pan by pressing a dull pencil gently into the metal.

Linda Masternak Justice • Kansas City, MO

Bug and Wing Patterns

Use with "Buggy Fan" on page 167.

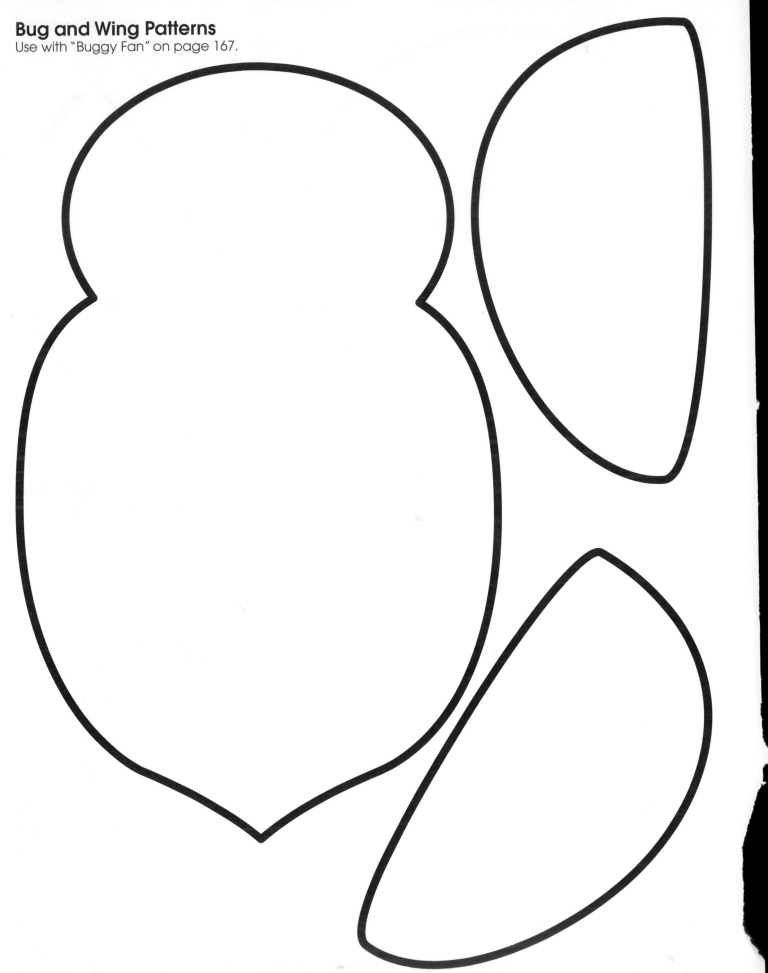

Eye Patterns
Use with "Tongue-Flicking Frog" on page 168.

Cut out.

Frog Pattern
Use with "Stand-Up Frog" on page 169.

Sun Patterns

Use with "Fiesta Sun" on page 173.